Table of Contents

Introduction

INTRODUCTION
Exploring Different Ideas

This book explores various ideas of what is happening on the court and will provide improvement solutions for players to improve their game. It is very important when coaching to analyze players by certain tips that are specific to why, how and what. These aspects are involved on the tennis court when a player is hitting and trying to win points. How are players making mistakes? Why are players making mistakes? What do players have to do to change to improve and win matches? A good coach is one who can pick out mental, physical and/or technical flaws and distinguish the instinctive (feel) vs. mechanical (physics) of a player's game. To further my method of exploring different ideas within this book, I have players look at and learn tennis sequences to help maximize their potential to hit the right shot at the right time. My purpose for this book is to encourage players on all levels of the game and to help train them to become better and more structurally sound players.

Try not to over-complicate the game. Simplicity is the key to great tennis, and it is easy to get overwhelmed. Many players soon find themselves not liking tennis, because of its complexity, and they often quit before giving themselves a chance. If a player wants to improve, it is better to go to a local pro to find a base or common ground for oneself as a tennis player and to not try not to do it all by oneself. Players should have a vision of where they want to see themselves playing as future players, whether it is professionally, as a local tournament player or as a social player. It helps for them to imagine how they can maximize their potential and for what purpose.

Making of Champions

It is advantageous for players to have different gears to reset themselves when they are not feeling 100% on court. Having routine shot patterns will increase their chances of delivering winning styles of play. It is also important to note that many players do not always trust themselves to hit a shot, because they feel they might be choosing the wrong shot to hit at a precise moment. The more dependable instinctive skills will come from neuro-muscle memory with disciplined repetition of shot patterns all over the court. Utilizing skills and maximizing potential comes by playing smart tactical tennis and incorporating it into players' game styles. Players should build confidence with a variety of shots and selections and by repeatedly practicing them. These actions will help them perform at their highest personal levels.

It is important for players to double-check their instincts to make sure their decisions match the scenario. As players know it is easy to be caught making bad choices after hitting the ball, as they often wish they could take it back and hit the ball in another direction. It is always important to remember that playing high percentage tennis is the first step. Playing the game with low percentage shot selections, such as going down the line with or hitting the greater degree of change, will hinder the winner percentage for a player. Smart tennis is the best tennis, especially when a player is struggling with the game.

Chapter 1 Not All Coaches Are the Same

When it comes to tennis instruction, it is best to get that training from good tennis coaches. Although there are commonalities in tennis, the way tennis is taught from one coach to the next is different. I have definitely seen and experienced this in my career. These differences have caused me to adapt my game many times to different coaches' ideas or takes on my game and the game as a whole. Some were very empowering, while others were less helpful, but I still managed to learn something from each. I found myself wondering if it was possible to find a coach that had all the best combinations of the good, so there was minimal negative impact on my game. Look for those coaches who are positive and motivating, who can pick out players' mental, physical and/or technical flaws, and who are able to distinguish the instinctive (feel) vs. mechanical (physics) of a player's game. Those are the ones who will help players develop to their highest potential more quickly.

In this project, I hope to compel my readers to think about tennis more than ever before, as a good coach would. Whether we agree to disagree or not, the fact remains there is a simple way to swing a racquet at a tennis ball, and it is there to grasp. I have discovered that if a person develops a specific start and a consistent finish that does not involve complex movement, a player will develop faster and become better over time than those having worked with multiple coaches with ever changing techniques.

One issue to be concerned about is counter body movements. These movements are what hinder a player's ability to develop strength in hitting a ball well with accuracy to place a ball. A player will be able to develop a consistent stroke once he or she realizes how simple it can be with the right techniques.

Chapter 2 Developing the Right Player within Oneself

I think it is important for players to ask themselves what kind of tennis players they are. Players who have been playing tennis for at least ten to twenty years probably already have an idea of what type of players they are, and hopefully they are good ones too. The purpose of this question is to help define one's game on the court, and to determine what makes a person a better player. Am I a better striker, a better runner or a better thinker on court? I have players question themselves so that they can better understand who they are on court and how they play.

The next question I have players ask themselves is, "Can I improve?" I advise tennis advocates and enthusiasts to always learn from the game and continue learning. Most of the time, players will tell me that they never come to the net, and there is no need to, because most of the points are always won on the baseline. Well, they are not wrong, but are simply misguided, because practicing other aspects of the game helps improve players' overall game, and it teaches players about their opponents. If players are able to put themselves in their opponent's shoes and know what weakness and strengths their opponents have, tennis matches can usually be won before a ball is ever hit. In addition, if players believe they are the best players out there, and they know how to win based on their time-won strategy, their confidence in winning matches can give them the mental edge they need. These players have already put in the time with their consistent practices with their structurally sound techniques and body positioning. They know how to move and to hit the ball with accuracy anywhere on the court. Always keep things simple, make tennis as simple as possible when playing the game.

Chapter 3 Tennis Can be Simple by Hard Work

Every person is born with different gifts. Some gifts are natural such as kicking a ball really well or another person can tell about Albert Einstein's theory of motion. The underlying fact is that people are born with different coordination skills. Some people can play sports better than others and not work as hard at it. When it comes to tennis, it can be challenging for a person who lacks the "natural talent" ability to play well. The question that I then propose players ask themselves is how badly they want to become really good tennis players? How badly do they want to win this match right now? How badly do they want to hit the tennis ball over the net? If most people desire a goal, then it is achievable. I have seen first-hand that players do not have to be a hundred percent coordinated to hit a tennis ball and be successful. This is the difference between being talented and players who are putting in the time and extra effort to develop their talent. Both types of players can win.

The "Working Talent"
(Even Professionals that play at the highest level in the game can benefit).

How do players achieve the "working talent?" The answer is quite simple, by the laws of physics. Players who have structured, consistent strokes where they have complete control over their minds and bodies will hit better strokes than players who waffle or keep changing between strokes. To conquer the game of tennis people have to visualize what type of players they want to become and match those ideas with their goals and adapt. There are going to be times when players do decide whether a two handed backhand is a better fit than a one handed backhand or vice versa. So what is the "working talent?" The working talent is to verify that players' swings and their motions are one hundred percent accurate so when they swing, they are swinging correctly and not using bad judgment based off instincts that will misguide the ball.

Chapter 4 The Broken "Mental" Technique

Errors come from uncertainty when players are uncertain as to how they should continue, and what shots they should hit and where to hit them. When players hit tennis balls in a match, their timing will eventually break down if they are not technically and structurally sound (Working Talent). Eventually, one of the players will miss during a rally point. The player who misses first will most likely be the player with what I call "the broken technique." So what is broken technique in terms of the physics of tennis? A broken technique is a player's inability to hit a ball over a three foot or three foot six inch net and land it in a seventy-eight foot court more often than their opponent. Angles of a racquet combined with the velocity of a swing make it difficult to create a consistent swing every time players hit the ball. So how does a player become consistent on court?

On the tennis court the mind is the most important asset to a player with all the "tools." A player that has all the tools is the player who can hit all the shots on the tennis court. One major difference between players who can have all the tools is their "mental game." For social players the mind can interfere and hinder their learning capability. Why does that happen and what does this mean? It happens most often to new players, because they learn tennis based on feel. Later on, the same set of players will have a difficult time adjusting to the control, pace and spin of shots that constantly get them off balance. Players often hit a tennis ball over the net without taking into account how their body is creating a shot. So the question we then ask is, "How consistent will I be when I advance in the future?" The best thing players can do is to be coached from the beginning and with the right physical and mental training to develop that consistency and success.

Chapter 5 Accepting the Difficult Times

The hardest part for adults to accept is failure, but failure is part of growing or learning. To be successful in tennis players have to up their games as they learn from their mistakes. For example, if players keep missing their serves, they must adjust, improve their strokes and practice consistently so that their hits go to the right place. In order to win they have to change and grow. How long will players serve with a "pancake" before they realize that there is no form nor technical balance in that shot? A "pancake grip" is simplistic shot, but it does not enhance a player's future, because it lacks power, and, therefore, it does not help a person's game in the long run. Players may eventually grow tired of getting beat by their opponents, and then they will finally change their serves and other strokes. However, by this time it may be too late as their personal feelings and thoughts may be warring with the coaches' ability to teach them now. This is not the players' fault, but the players' minds, because their minds have concluded that they had already tried to hit the ball this way or that way, and it did not work out. We all need to be willing to adapt and change to improve with positive mental focus and practice. I also have had to change my grips, because my balance and technique were off. I did not realize it those times, because I did not have the insight to identify those mistakes when I was younger. Accepting that it is the right thing to do is important when making changes in one's game depending upon what goals a player may have. When the mind is young on the tennis court, it goes by instinct, not mechanical thoughts. If players have the physics of how to hit every ball properly, their confidence will build around the mechanics of tennis and help make them champions.

Chapter 6 The Proper Mindset to Approach a Technique

This chapter will focus on the fundamentals of tennis and how to stay structural sound on the court. The kinetic chain, the mind and the timing are all prominent aspects of a tennis stroke. The development of tennis players is often inconsistent with reasons varying from different tennis coaches to different sizes and shapes of players' bodies. If players use a complex variation to hit a tennis ball, it will consist of many different parts. Sometimes, players' strokes are not structural sound; they do not have the same take back with the racquet or swing and follow through on a consistent basis, because their technique is too complex.

It is true that tennis players including top professionals may have different grips or swings to hit balls, but the simplistic art of hitting a tennis ball will dedicate itself to hitting with limited movement and with perfect form. If there is one thing that will help prove this, it is with the laws of physics and vectors.

How can a player win matches with an unorthodox swing? What may work for one player may not work for another. If players decide to go outside the laws of physics to hit a ball, chances are they are hurting themselves, because they will not be able to control the tennis ball enough times to win matches in the long run. Unorthodox styles are hard to compete with at a high level, because their inconsistency usually is a hindrance once power comes into play. The more power a player hits on the ball, the less control an unorthodox player will have, because the power will out-play the unorthodox style. Extreme western grips are an example of an unorthodox style. However, once a player becomes so unorthodox that players cannot figure out how to play against the person, it can become an advantage until the other player can overpower the unorthodox style. The objective on the tennis court is to figure out how to win twelve games with a player's tools before his or her opponent does.

Chapter 7 The Tools of a Player

Players often know what their strengths and weaknesses are and sometimes know their opponents.' Many people tend to not focus on their own game (tools) well enough to maximize their winning potential. What I mean is that many players do not focus on winning their serves within four easy points. Instead, they most likely will grind out four points, if not go to deuce multiple times before losing or holding serve. If players want to win tournaments or events, they will have a tough time grinding their way through a tournament rather than easing their way with their own tools into the finals.

"Difference of Playing the Game and Winning at Tennis"

Many players have a tendency to want to improve, but do not necessarily care enough to win matches. Recreational players enjoy the game just enough that they will improve to be able to play at a level they are comfortable with, but it may not be a winning game. If that is what makes players happy, then that is okay. On the other side it is hard to accept losses. Players then ask themselves why they are not winning their matches. Some players really do need to change their game a lot, but they do not want to backtrack after many years of playing. This is a hard concept to deal with. It is hard for players to tell themselves that they definitely want to improve, but then they go back to the routine strokes they have been using for years. This is when it is important to commit to change for the right reasons. If players truly want to gain tools or a single strength on court, they must fix the flaw. Even some professionals have flaws they do not want to change, because they do not want to start over or create mental chaos on court. Nevertheless, if players really listen and follow through with these next chapters, their game can grow dramatically, and they will feel so much better on court. The more tools players have to work with, the better their chances are at winning matches.

"Having the Right Tools"

Players' greatest strengths will be their tools and only their tools. The key is to see what tools a player can use to dictate a point. For most players it is their forehand hitting deep, with either a lot of pace or spin. For some others it is closing the net or serving aces. It needs to be stressed that it is not only crucial for players to master a tool or tools, but they should also learn how to break others' strengths down, when they observe them. If players have big serves, how are their opponents going to get in their heads to take it away? If they have good footwork, how do their opponents jam them or test their conditioning to get them off balance? Always remember that strengths will break down, if players are not used to being stressed. Stress forces players to get uncomfortable and mix up their game. So what strengths should players choose to develop? Players should look for the shots that they are most comfortable hitting, and then they should check to see if that shot generates the most pace (power). The "power shots" players hit will come from the area where they are flattening out their shots or generating the most pace. If players' forehand is their favorite shot to hit, but they are not beating their opponents with it, it may be that the stroke has too many complex variables, meaning they are hitting off balance. When players hit off balance, they are losing pace and accuracy. This also most likely means that their opponents are playing more consistently. Remember, the more unorthodox the stroke is, the more inconsistent it will be against other power players. In regards to power players they may be able to hit a great forehand at fifty miles per hour, but what about one hundred miles per hour, does their forehand change technically? The racquet length at which the amount of time players need to hit through their swings will dictate how well they can perform under pressure from powerful shots.

Chapter 8 "Tri-Force" in Tennis Theory

The balance, rhythm and power (B.R.P.) of tennis is a tri-force theory that will make a good player a great player at any level of the game. Balance is the undertone of rhythm and power, and without it, a person's stroke will break down. Balance is the centerpiece that holds a person's posture. When players have to move excessively, it becomes challenging to maintain proper balance, because their bodies get tired and sluggish. If the balance aspect breaks down, so will the rhythm and the power, and they will not be as accurate.

What is proper balance? When talking about the forehand, balance can be looked at as a propeller; in essence a plus sign (+). When a person stands upright, the most powerful and structurally balanced point would in fact be one hundred eighty degrees out away from the player's body. The challenge is to hit the ball at contact to give the stroke the best chance. Yes, variations of the stroke are going to happen, but keep in mind that the right principles on how to hit the tennis ball will generate the accuracy that many of the power players have been missing in their strokes. Another theory example of tri-force are the volleys. Hitting volleys at forty-five degrees while standing upright will give players greater balance and accuracy without moving their bodies. It is a big problem, when players hunch over and get off balance to hit their volleys. This is usually the first mistake newer or exhausted players make, and it necessary for them to correct their balance and footwork. If players were sitting in a chair while they volley, they would notice that their volleys are to the side and not in front. This stability from the body will give the volleying players much more accurate shots without moving as much as they may think it takes to hit the perfect volley. Overcompensating the volley happens most often when players get that volley they can put away, but it ends up going out or in the net. Remember to keep the balance aspect simple and smart, this will help develop into a player's rhythm on court.

Chapter 9 Rhythm

Rhythm is a great way of staying consistent and getting power on shots. If players hit without rhythm, they are more than likely to become sporadic players and make unforced errors. Hitting with rhythm will keep the ball consistently in the court. Knowing when to swing at the right time and at the precise moment is easier once players develop their balance. Once players have a consistent balance to hit the ball (what I like to call their base), they can connect with the rhythm or pace of the shot. Rhythm will dictate how much power players will need to hit the ball over the net into their opponent's court. If players do not have the proper rhythm, it could be because they are not in balance or their timing of contact from the racquet to the ball is off. Counting is one of the easiest ways to get into a rhythm. Different opponents and players will hit with a different pace. Some players may find it difficult to adjust to the speed of the ball. Sometimes it is because opponents hit with different spins or racquet head speed. On the other hand, it might even be that the surface is different, and the ball reacts slower or speeds up after making contact with the surface. No matter the case, finding a way to count after the opponent hits the ball, and when the other player makes contact with the ball will determine what I call a "base." This base is the player's rhythm and timing being developed and adapting to the speed of the opponent. It would be wise to count on multiple shots to make sure that the player's base is the "normal ball" being hit by the opponent. A player must remember to stay in balance, when timing the opponent's shot. Once the player is able to read the opponent's speed, the player's shots, which are now balanced with rhythm, will allow the player to hit more freely with power.

Chapter 10 Power

Players can never get enough power. Without power it is tough to be a great tennis player. Some people can "counterpunch" or never make a mistake and win some matches. However, players that just get the ball back into the court without a sense of power will have to grind their way to win matches. Power is the essential goal for most tennis enthusiasts. The more power there is, the greater the potential to win matches. When players have both balance and rhythm, power will come a lot easier to these players, because they will begin to feel the ball as it becomes a more consistent shot. To capitalize on the power think about it like a serve. Players can hit a big serve, when the toss is in the right spot, and their timing is perfect. It is no different on the groundstrokes, except players must return a ball that also has a lot of topspin and pace and is moving players all around the court. To make it easier, here are a few tips: 1) As I said before, think of hitting shots like a serve. There is no reason players cannot develop their groundstrokes as a "snap shot" to unleash a multitude of power. If their balance and rhythm are right, their power will come into the shot with a snap of a wrist. If players are pushing the ball and adding topspin at the last second, they have a long way to go, because they are pushing the ball with their arm, and that hinders their chances at maximum power. Players can also give themselves more complex variables with the more topspin they try to add to their shots, but for the power, it is best to stick to the basic one hundred eighty degrees flat. 2) Load like a + sign and try the one hundred eighty degree hit. Like a baseball or golf swing players see the body is straight and their arms are straight on contact. Remember to stay balanced and structured, so the power comes through on the shot. If players are moving around too much, their bodies release their power elsewhere, so players will not have as much strength to hit as they would have had, if they had stayed in an upright position. Once again it is about the "overcompensating" factor.

Chapter 11 The Key to Why Player Make Mistakes and the Overcompensating Factor

Many players like to move, bend, overrun and play their hearts out on court. I wish I could say I like all these aspects in a player as they remind me of a hard worker on court. However, many talented young players waste their energy on bad tennis. What I mean here is that many players will overcorrect themselves to hit a good shot. For example, a player may lean back more, because they hit more topspin to let the ball drop deep, or they lean over to hit a kick serve with more topspin. Other examples are hitting a volley out in front (as stated earlier) to make the ball go over the net. Many players do not see the harm in their bodies by overcompensating to hit a shot, but what players should notice is that the high-level pros hit their powerful shots and stay balanced without much body movement. This is because they have mastered both balance and rhythm, and that creates their power. Those who move too much to hit a certain shot will drop their power level and create torsion. Torsion is when players' muscles are fighting each other within their bodies instead of working together to hit a fluid shot.

"How not to Overcompensate"

Tennis is played at many levels by talented athletes who use their physical and mental skills to hit a tennis ball. However, what many players do not realize is that most of the time; their physical movements are hindering their technical grasp of how to strike a tennis ball. In essence, tennis is based on trying to hit a ball that is traveling with a certain speed and velocity. To redirect the ball to where players want to hit it takes patience, time and energy. Like many players, a tennis player will hit a ball based on the "knowhow" or feel. Yes, players can hit a ball on the court and become great players by playing with techniques as they learn and develop. However, many tennis players are making tennis harder on themselves, because they are trying to correct a physical flaw within their game without understanding "why." For instance, a person hitting a forehand from a really low point must finish at a very high point in order to get the ball over the net and in the court with a topspin. That same player swings with the racquet starting low to high and back to low again. The player has now entered the "overcompensating factor." Overcorrecting a mistake is a very common development among tennis players. This habit runs counter the laws of simplicity on hitting balls in the tennis court. Feel most of the time counterbalances mathematical comfort ability, and it is hard to get out of a grove once a player feels comfortable with his or her stroke. So what is the solution? The best solution to take care of the issues is to watch films of oneself or others playing tennis, and having a coach there who can show players what to look for, and to point out logical reasons as to why the tennis ball is not moving where the players want it go. Another point is to start early. The earlier players are able to understand the correct swings without overcompensating or over-correcting their swings, the better those players chances of success on the tennis court.

Chapter 12 Movement and the Errors Tennis Players Make

Footwork is a key element in tennis, but it can also seriously hinder a player's ability to perform well on court as it affects a player's balance. If anyone has watched a pro tennis player play an amateur player in a tennis match, it quickly becomes obvious that the professional player is calmer. Professional players can hit the ball in almost an effortless form, and this creates far greater power behind the shots than the amateur player has whose feet are moving and running down every shot as if it was his or her last point. Great effort may come at a great cost for too many players. Just because players move their feet a lot, does not mean they are better. Their excessive movement may cost them the ability to hit the ball in the perfect state. Yes, moving to the ball is essential, but there is no need to move to the ball and overcompensate for a ball that just needs to be struck well. One solution to this is calmness. Staying calm helps relax a player and relinquishes the tenseness in the body that may affect a player's ability to strike a ball. Never give up great form for bad movement. Other notes that players need to remember is not to take too many steps. Sometimes, one player just takes one extra step, and that in some matches is all it takes to lose when two players are dead even in terms of skill and stamina. Taking a step back instead of forward or talking an extra step to change directions often hurts players on court. The best way to hit a tennis ball is by understanding the steps it takes to hit and still be balanced while moving. If that concept is too difficult to understand, players will try their setup position which is approximately their final three steps before hitting the ball. There is one step that most players do not even know exists, but they need to utilize, and that is the "after step" on the volleys. Most players will step into a volley without striking the ball first. This process just sent most of the players' energy and power into the ground, leaving only what power the players have left to hit with just their arms.

Chapter 13 The After Step for Volleys

The "after step" is one of the most crucial forms in tennis and many players make the mistake of not using it correctly. On volleys, many players tend to step in before or at the same time as hitting the ball and making contact with the ball. In reality, players should make contact with the racquet and then step into the shot as a player's weight is being transferred through the shot. When players hit the volley with the racquet next to their bodies, they have a better chance to control the volley and the speed of the ball. This helps players with their stability and coordination. Players who step in and then hit tend to be off balance and loose energy. Players that hit at a higher level will hit before stepping, because the ball has traveled so fast, so the only way to hit it is with the racquet first. With that being said, staying balanced with the body is a key element to hitting a solid volley. For example, a backhand volley tends to be the harder volley to hit. Players that have trouble with this volley need to look at hitting a left-handed forehand volley, but with two hands. Using the left side of players' bodies, their left hands will naturally set up a forty-five degree angle. Their elbows should be able to give them enough distance from their bodies to stay both in balance and stay within the forty-five degree range. Early preparation is necessary for groundstrokes, but it is also a key element when volleying. Early preparation will increase the players' chances of being balanced and being able to move closer to the net for higher percentage hits. It is important to remember that the after step is not a late step, but, rather, is a step of balance when a player's body weight transfers into the volley. Therefore, when players go for that backhand volley, they must turn their shoulders first, let the ball contact the racquet as they are shifting their weight into the shot, and then step.

Chapter 14 Controlling Speed and Time

It is important for players to hit a ball faster than the ball coming into their stroke. An example of this is if a player is hitting to his or her opponent at ten miles per hour, the opponent should hit the ball at about fifteen miles per hour to gain control of the tennis ball, otherwise the opponent will lose the ability to control the tennis ball. It is important to control the ball, because if the player does not control the ball, the shot will not be accurate to where the player intended to hit it to. It is important not to play on the defensive side of power, because the player's opponent will realize when the opposing side is weaker at hitting. Any sign of weakness of player playing on the defensive will add confidence and aggressiveness to the power player. However, there is hope for players who do not play with a lot of pace or speed, and that is the factor of "time."

"Time"

Controlling time on the tennis court will give players the benefit of controlling matches that are not easy to win. If players are having a difficult time getting and creating power, understand that taking away the opposing side's time by getting to the net is crucial. Perhaps a player may be more comfortable taking a ball on the rise instead of coming to the net. Alternatively, going to the net in general will help eliminate being run off the court by players with more powerful strokes. Tennis is about time. How much time does a player have to recover on the court? How much time does it take to get to the net before the ball comes back? If a player is able to control time, that player will be able to control a match. Players need to also realize that with a long wind up (swing), they must give themselves more time to implement the topspin and power. If players do not do this, then the ball will be misdirected and the shot will be off the projected target.

Chapter 15 The Instinctive Side vs. Mechanical Side (Technique)

What I am writing in this chapter is going to be the hardest for most players, because this is about one of the biggest flaws in players' games. Sometimes players' instincts are telling them to hit into a ball in a certain way, and they continue to hit this way, because they feel they need too; they are comfortable with it. It is understandable that players want to stick with a swing that they have used for years. However, if the stroke is causing more harm than good, why keep using it? For example, why would a person keep a car with old parts that breaks down all the time instead of using a more reliable vehicle? Players should focus on using reliable swings. They should open their eyes to the possibility that, if they watch videos or films of themselves playing tennis, they should be able to notice mathematical errors such as unstable angles and changes in the consistency of their strokes. In those videos, players can also see how they move prior to hitting the ball. If their instinct is spot on, then their mechanical side or technical side will soon follow with good shots. If they miss hitting the shot, there could be a problem with their pace or rhythm. Their rhythm could have a spot that is breaking down and needs to be examined. It is important to note that players' instinct will not always be accurate, and until they have trained significantly with the proper mechanics/techniques, they will find themselves in a whirlwind of training, but with gaining only minimal ground. Therefore, those who focus on the mechanics and vectors of how they are hitting the balls will be able to watch their game grow immensely. An important lesson here is for players to see themselves swing on video, and then they will be able to tell what movements are helping or hindering their swing.

Chapter 16 Developing Power towards Swinging Away

As players learn and grow they will notice that their level of tennis will change. The more powerful players will become more consistent and begin to win more matches. Power strikers (flatter hitters) will become more of a deciding factor in the game. Sure, topspin does help get the ball in the court, but unlike the junior circuit, the power game becomes the ruler in the higher levels of the game. It becomes very rare to find players that drop shot and use short angle shots to win matches. Players with more power will hit more deeply and will consistently keep their opponents on their back feet. There is a much greater advantage in being a hard hitter with depth than a topspin hitter with control at the higher levels. What people do not realize is that hitting a topspin shot has more variables and will become a more complex shot over time. When players hit with topspin, they are sacrificing power and accuracy. Hitting flatter one hundred eighty degree hits will develop the most power over time. The harder part for players is in controlling the power while they are developing it, and that is what the balance and rhythm are for. With the proper timing of their shots, and staying in balance, players will find that controlling power has just become a whole lot easier. No player always hits powerful balls one hundred percent of the time in seventy-eight foot courts, but winning more free points and controlling the match sounds a whole lot better than grinding for hours. Once players have mastered the balance, rhythm and the power, they can now work their way to the zone.

Chapter 17 Getting Into the Zone

Players often define the zone as a place where they can hit their shots all day long, or they describe it as the best they have ever played. The zone is a place where players feel they can hit anything and beat anyone on even given day on the court. On those days every shot in the book is theirs. The zone is a place where everything players hit goes in, and they can play at about any point on the court. To get to the zone in tennis players must be able to reach a point of trusting all of their strokes both mechanically and instinctively. As a result, simple errors would not frustrate these players, because they believe that every ball from them will land where they choose. When playing a match, strong players can start strong and learn to not get frustrated, because the ball will eventually fall in once the players enter the zone in the match. Other players who have a harder time trusting themselves should take this approach, the "Ladder Approach," to get into the zone. I say this because more often than not, spectators will see players play one great game or a series of great games, but then lose the match. What happened here? Players could find fatigue a huge factor. For instance, if players start strong, but then weaken after an hour of playing, they may not be in the greatest shape to hit all of their shots. Another factor is the players' mental game. Many times, I have seen players play great games and then retreat to hitting with too much caution, causing them to loose matches they should be winning. Lastly, players simply do not know how to sustain the same strategy to beat their opponents, and then they begin to over-think points. It is important for players to trust themselves and their shots, as the more confidence players have, the more mentally ready they will be for their match.

"Tips to the zone"

I hear from players that they have good days and bad days. This tells me that they have relied more on instinctive tennis instead of mechanical tennis. Once the mechanics are set into place, players should not struggle with good or bad days unless they are mentally distracted. Ideally, players should be able to get into the zone by obtaining enough practice both mentally and physically on court to prepare for their matches. For the first game on the return of their serves, just getting the ball back into play whether it is with slicing or short swings will help. I am not saying that this is the proven way to break the opponent, but it is, rather, the way for players to let themselves get a feel for the zone and work towards that. After getting a few balls in, they can then set themselves for a more medium pace swing. After winning their serves, they can either wait for another game to get into the zone, or they can start swinging away. Pros in the zone hit with great correctness. When pros are not in the zone in all of their shots, it may be because they are not always in the right striking area. However, they adjust, because they have acquired through much training and practice the talent to get back into the zone and to find their balance, rhythm and power.

Chapter 18 Playing Live Matches vs. Practice Matches

Playing a live match can be one of the toughest scenarios for players to be in. When players have not been winning their matches that day, spectators often ask why the players did not win. The easiest answer is that the players need to practice more "live" match play. Practice makes perfect, but only if players practice the right things, not the wrong things. If one of the goals of players is to be the best "practice grinders," they will only be as good as their bodies support this. Practicing more match (live) play will help with nerves and situations that do not arise in practice. Practicing without absorbing the proper live match play will hinder the learning experience, because many people are intimidated by playing in front of people they do not know. This is like being a great singer at home, but being too nervous to sing in front of people. It is best for players to play at least one or two matches a week with strangers, if they are playing regularly. If players can, they should play in two tournaments a month to help with the transition from practice to live matches. Once they get to the zone, players cease worrying about nerves. The zone takes players to a place of concentration where their minds will only be focused on tennis and nothing else. It is important for players to have a clear vision of what they hope to achieve on the court and follow that path to their goals on the court. They should set themselves up to concentrate and ignore distractions. If they are thinking about other things, they must find their ways to concentrate, whether it is by watching tennis videos or tennis games, hitting balls or concentrating on their footwork. Music can be a relaxing thing that does calm people, however, music is also a distraction from the job at hand, and that is getting to the zone. If players' heads are filled with music as tennis is about to play, then they are not prepared to go into battle unless they ultimately need a distraction to help stay calm.

Chapter 19 Mental: Anticipation and Developing Court Sense

"The Art of Anticipation"

If players do not know where the ball is coming from, they will not be ready, and they will be unset. Yes, players can react to the ball, but eventually, they will be over-powered and their reaction time will not be quick enough to win the point. Knowing where the ball is going ahead of time increases the probability that players' movements mean everything will piece together and will be more precise rather than their movements being scrambled on court. It is essential to study opponents' games to get a better feel for their timing and strokes.

"Natural Talent/Movement"

Natural movers that play tennis have a great sense of knowing where to be on court. They instinctively know where to go based on the shot they hit, as they have learned what to expect in return. For an easy example, if a ball drops at players' feet when they are up at the net, a drop shot is to be anticipated by their opponents, thus leading to the original players running forward before their opponents hit the ball. This is what we would call "court sense." So how does a person develop court sense? Well the obvious answer is to play a lot of tennis and play the percentages of what can be known as "knowledgeable tactics." If players hit a nice deep crosscourt ball, the ball will most likely be returned crosscourt. If a ball lands short, most likely opponents will go up the line unless they like their inside out shot or cannot hit the ball up the line. To develop court sense it is wise for players to start small with knowledgeable tactics. In this way players can build anticipation with their court sense and therefore, stop relying on reaction shots as players play more match play scenarios.

"How to Become a Mind Reader on Court"

Knowing the opponents' game makes tennis easier to play. Combine this with the knowledge of how tennis should be played at the highest level, and it allows for easy anticipation scenarios to present themselves during matches. One basic rule to start with is to let opponents go for low percentage shots. If players lose points to players who are taking the low percentage, that is not a bad day, because, eventually, the opponents will fall into a trap. Once opponents hit one low percentage shot in, they will tend to go for those shots repeatedly. Their moves are easier to anticipate after that one play. It may not feel like it, but it is better for opponents to win a few low percentage shots. Just do not let these points affect you. However, there are players that need to win every point and every match. For those individuals they have a long road ahead. The outcome of the match is typically dictated by the person who makes fewer errors. If there is a fundamental technical difference between a pro and a recreational player, it is the thought that the recreational player will not win the match, because the pro looks like a better player. If they regularly have a hard time with getting into themselves on court (overthinking), I always tell my players to play the ball more often than the opponent. However, if two players are evenly matched, the smarter opponent will usually win, because of smarter one's anticipation of plays, or as I like to say, "Staying ahead." Staying at least one or two steps ahead helps smooth out the point, so the planner will not mishit as often, which typically happens to players that just hit the ball and plan on staying ahead in their points.

Chapter 20: Asking "Why" for Matches and Points

I decided to add this note, because players need to understand the importance of tennis matches. When players are young, it is nice to have quick matches and get into the finals as quickly as possible. Since tennis is such a young person's sport, it is important to learn very quickly to absorb as much knowledge from every match. Scores do not matter unless the player wants them to matter, and playing well and not playing well does not matter either. At that time, tennis players need to understand what they are doing to win and lose every point they play. If they mishit a ball, why did it mishit? If they were passed, why did they get passed? If they double faulted, why? Always ask why, and it is surprising how fast bad habits go away. Another notion here about being steady is that players will not win every point they play, but the better they get, players will find themselves asking, "Why not?" It is important to be a good loser in tennis, because unlike other sports, there is only one winner. Having a 1 in 32, 64, or 128 chance of winning is slim, and that is without talking about qualifying for a tennis tournament. Not to play devil's advocate, but many tennis players need to understand very early on that loosing matches is just as important as winning matches in the early stages. From this training period, players will emerge by winning a lot more matches or know how to win matches against players that they have lost to in their earlier days. Also important is to always leave with something positive from matches, like a player's court sense, own development, shot selection or any other working ideas players are working towards. Therefore, never underestimate the power of why when playing on court.

Chapter 21 Technology

Tennis enthusiasts should be careful when developing their game on court. Many players that talk to me about issues they are having on court have lighter, developing racquets (nine ounces). These beginners need to try a heavier racquet first, and they will soon see that it helps, as they begin to notice the rest of their bodies swinging into the shot. Those players who rely on their arms to hit the ball all day will overwork their muscles too quickly and will break down sooner rather than later, whether it is physically or mentally. So what am I suggesting here in technology? Tennis players that are serious about tennis should get a midsize eleven ounce racquet when playing. This type of racquet is not too heavy or too light for starting out. It is surprising how much more control and how much quicker players will learn when they use a heavier racquet. In addition, a smaller head size around ninety-eight inches is good for those in training. Training correctly from the beginning will help players develop faster rather than more slowly with great frustration. Light racquets have too much of a trampoline effect that causes less accurate shots and less feel from the racquet. Another question that presents itself a lot is what racquet is going to be better in the future?

When players discover their game style, they find their racquet. It is hard to start with a racquet and know that racquet is going to be the only stick for the next ten years. Players that are starting out can develop their game style based on the racquet that they choose, because their instincts will tell them what shot to hit when, based on feel. Feel is so crucial in tennis because that is how players develop their habits, because they subconsciously are adjusting to what the ball is going to do after it makes contact with the racquet. A simple idea here would be, if you like to swing big, go a bit heavier. The shorter the swing, the smaller the ounce of the racquet.

Chapter 22 The Mechanical Chair

In this section, I am only going to talk about the mechanics in the physical sense and not the ones that repair vehicles. Tennis like anything takes attention, like attention to one's body, and how it reacts to a tennis ball is crucial in understanding oneself as a player. If players are not hitting the ball cleanly, perhaps it is time for them to take a different approach and train their bodies better. By utilizing the ideas of kinesiology, everything in tennis works together like a chain. It is best to say that if people have control of the chain, they will be able to hit any tennis shot they want. Remember the "zone." I will give the one example I gave earlier in this book and that would be the "chair position." When players are getting into the ready position at the net, a lot of them are leaning forward and are bracing themselves for a volley, or they react to a volley. It is crucial to understand that leaning forward is not a natural position for the body, especially when trying to react to a tennis ball coming at the body. Since volleys are hit to players' sides, they will notice that their bodies feel and look more stable in a chair position. When players bend their legs in from of their bodies, they have already put their bodies in the proper stance to react to a ball. If players simply turn their shoulders to the left or too the right, they will notice that they are still in a balanced position. This position will prepare players to hit without moving their feet. When players are leaning forward, they have to move back and adjust their feet to get into position. However, by this time, the ball has already gotten to them, and they will not be able to react with a counter shot the way they would hope to. Remember, the more simplistic players are, the easier life will be on the court.

Chapter 23 Developing a Technique

To develop a technique players have to know what type of players they would like to become. If they want to become one of the best players in the world, they need to develop power. If players are hoping to be recreational players, they should learn how to control the ball with the topspin. Even with hoping to hit at the highest level, it helps to develop a player's game early and hitting flat will help players grow. Power is the ultimate goal in tennis! The more power and free points players win will dictate not only the matches they are playing, but also their future matches in tournaments. Rather than grinding and pushing the ball back for three hours, try to find a way to win free points in the game to ease the burden of long matches. If developing power is a problem for players, they should see what grip they are using and should remind themselves to check their balance, rhythm and power. This will help with flatting out the shot to one hundred eighty degrees to give them the greatest power. Keep in mind, there are different grips in tennis that pertain to different weapons people can develop as players.

If players play with a lot of spin, they will be okay. It is not necessary that a player use a continental grip to obtain the best power shot, because there is a height difference between the net and the actual height of a player. It is important to always understand "B.R.P.," because players will find themselves going in circles trying to figure out why some shots are going in and why some are going out. If players are looking to me to tell them which shot is the best, I will tell them to see for themselves by understanding that all the grips have something to give but also something that may hinder a player's performance. Remember as I said earlier, if power is the players' ultimate goal, they need to remind themselves of the complex variables at hand to hit the ball as they continue their journeys to becoming the best players they can be.

Different technical forms of tennis game styles:

Forehand Grip: Advantages

Continental
1. Adaptable to serve and volley
2. Degree of versatility
3. Adaptable to serve
4. Easy to hit 180° Flat
5. Play inside the baseline
Eastern:
1.Able to Hit flat at 180° of Power
2. Less Variables
3. Balanced Ground Strokes
4. Small change on return of serve
Semi Western
1.High amount of topspin
2. Disguise
3. Returning with topspin 4.Court surface Adaptability
5. Shot can still be hit flat at different angle
Western:

1. Most Topspin
2. Sharper Angles
3. Topspin Lob
4. Play behind the base line
5. Most rotations during topspin of any grip

Forehand Grip: Disadvantages base on variable change when holding the racquet
Continental: Lowest level of variable change
Eastern: Minimal level of complex variables of change
Semi Western: Medium level of complex variable change
Western: Highest level of complex variable change

Chapter 24 The Robotic Rotation

The body is a crucial part of playing tennis, as great power comes from the rotation of the body. When players give their bodies the best coiling position to uncoil, it will help with sustaining the balance and power in their shots. As in the section earlier talking about the chair and players just turning their shoulders, players will notice that control often comes from their bodies. Think of the body as a plain. As players rotate the top half of their bodies, they are allowing themselves to wind up as a pitcher would to throw a ball. When players come through with their playing arm going straight out, they will see it produce a similar angle both above and below the arm. If players hit a tennis ball with the same angle straight at the point of connect, they will notice the control and power difference in their shots.

"Be a Robot on Court"

It is not often that players do not see themselves making easy mistakes. When players see other players hit a tennis ball, they are normally watching the ball. As coaches, we are watching everything else but the ball. Great coaches understand that how the body is reacting and not reacting to the tennis ball matters. It is safe to assume that a robot is the closest thing to a perfect tennis player. If robots could only move vertically and horizontally and never change their swings, how often would they miss? It is true that they may have trouble will low balls, but if they took every ball on the rise or break down their opponent for never missing a power consistent ball, that would be a tough player to beat. Remember players, trying to win one hundred percent of the points is not true tennis. Winning just over fifty percent is.

Chapter 25 Simplifying the 45° on Volleys

If players are planning to hit clean volleys, players need to try to build into the concept of the robot. Be aware that this disregards a lot of previous teachings of the game of tennis. Hitting a volley with the idea of a "one hundred-eighty degree straight-arm at a forty-five degree angle" creates balance and accuracy as long as the player is not hitting out in front. Swinging or moving with a ball at one hundred miles per hour is very tough, so why should players do any extra work that might decrease their margin of error? Punching volleys and hitting volleys in front of themselves are terms that players have probably heard before. By the way, "Do not do it!" What players need to know is that by not hitting volleys out in front of themselves, but at their sides allows more stability and balance, and will result in a much cleaner and more accurate volley. For stabilization, volleying with players' bodies instead of just their arms helps control the ball. Moving through the ball with their footwork instead of swinging or chopping at the ball will help with their balance. Remember the chair stance in the earlier chapter. Players should pretend they are sitting in the chair. They should put their playing arm out to the side at one hundred eighty degrees and their wrist cocked at a forty-five degree angle. If that is too hard to do, they may also shorten the volley by tucking their inner elbow to their sides and extending their arms out at a forty-five degree angle and their wrists will follow suit. Both of these shots are where the volleys need to be hit at the point of contact for stability and control of players' shots.

Example1: Backhand Volley ___

Example 2: Forehand Volley ___/

To tie volleying together with the after step in the earlier chapter, players should volley with only moving their feet to develop the proper after step. After the ball has made contact with their racquets, their movement should have already prompted their movement forward. Players' weight moving forward will force them to take a step forward, hence, "the after step." If players choose not to step, because they are stopped in their tracks, they may still feel their body's movement going from their back to their front foot. This is a correct body weight transfer. If players are not feeling this movement, they should try rocking their weight back and forth. Coaches instructing players should tell their players that they should stay on their back foot, hit, and then step forward. If players are having trouble, they should allow themselves to rock back and forth while they are being fed forehand volleys. They will start to feel the volley contact point when they are on their back foot transferring their weight. It is important for them to remember that they do not want their front foot to touch the ground before they make contact with the ball, or they will lose the power in the shot unless they are trying to hit a drop shot or another advanced shot.

Chapter 26 The Zero Degree Change (Δ)

When players hit a serve, they can hit at any angle they choose. Many servers tend to wind up too soon and loose power on their serve. A lot of players make the mistake of using their whole entire body to go after a ball which conflicts with the kinetic chain. Instead, players must realize that, like throwing a ball, their dominate right or left arm has to be relaxed and not create a conflict with other parts of the body. Since so many players start their hits early, their body weight brings down the upper body before the arm has a complete motion through the ball which causes a loss in power and direction. Staying upright for as long as possible and throwing the arm at the body instead of the body moving forward will enhance a player's success after developing a natural swing. Players who practice these moves will develop great form over time. Players who have never played tennis before, ideally, should be able to gather greater learning techniques and eliminate future bad habits, so they will be able to serve well and accurately. Unlike the forehand and backhand being hit with a degree of change, a server is able to hit at any angle without a degree of change.

The importance of hitting the tennis ball with a zero degree of change: Serving is one of the best strokes of the game, because the servers gets to control where they can serve without changing directions. When players are in a rally, they have to change directions multiple times and that can lead to unforced errors. Many players do not know that when they hit a ball straight back in the same direction it came from, that is a zero degree of change. Having said that, when a player is standing on the baseline in singles, a nineteen degree of change is the maximum degree of change a player wants to hit if they are hitting crosscourt after a ball was hit down the line to them. If players are at net, they are looking at a thirty-eight degree of change from the top of the net from one baseline corner to the other baseline corner. Doubles is a little larger with a twenty-four degree of change from down the line to cross-court and a forty-nine degree of change at the center of the net. It is important that if a player gets a ball that is faster or slower, it will affect the degree at which the players' racquet is facing. Why is this information significant? To truly understand tennis and how it works it is important to know that when players change the direction of the ball, they are adding a risk factor by contributing a greater angle when they make contact with the ball. Hitting that ball back the same direction it came from is a zero degree of change, and that is crucial to know when deciding which shot a player needs to hit next. If people wonder why players like to hit down the line when an opponent approaches up the line, it is because of zero degree Δ. It is important to also understand that when players are not hitting the tennis ball as well as they would like, they should check to see if they are trying to develop a rhythm while staying at zero degrees. They should look to see if they are generating too many obtuse angles on their shots, and perhaps they will see themselves becoming players that are more consistent. Hitting at zero degree of change will help players stay in control, and they also should check to make sure their balance, rhythm, and power are connecting on court. The degree of change is one great factor that is undermined, but can transcend a good player to a great player as it paves the way towards the path to playing smarter tennis.

Chapter 27 Examples of Playing Smart Tennis (S, D)

"Playing Smart Singles"

Players will always want to play smart tennis. For instance, with their serves players hope to wear down their opponents, so their opponents are moving all over the court. When a player is returning on a love-forty game, they do not need to scramble all around the court, because they know that they will be serving next game, and there is no need to start serving tired. Players should always remember their places and play the many situations that arise on the court.

"Playing Smart Doubles"

Crowding the net and letting the players go down the line is an awesome tactic to use on opponents. Players need to realize that giving opponents the highest part of the net and the shortest distance (down the line) is better than giving them the rest of the court, not to mention that the out of bounds is just outside of the alley as well. If players lose a match after playing high percentage tennis, they should not feel badly. Knowing that they will not win every match and every point is a hard pill to swallow. Players can always feel confident they will win matches playing high percentage tennis, but some matches are just not in the books to win in doubles. If the opponents are playing in the zone more than the other players are, it is going to be a tough match. Players can win every match they play, and yet feel like they made the wrong choices when they were hitting. It is very good to think about shot selections afterwards. Players should analyze their selections and ask why? If it made sense that they lost straight up, then they should not beat themselves up. If they are playing low percentage shots and not playing into their zones, then they have a right to be arguing with themselves over their choices. Keep in mind that players can lose a match and play smart, but they should be trying to give themselves the best possible chance to win on court and playing high percentage singles and doubles could do that for them.

Chapter 28 Doubles Strategy & Planning

Like many sports today tennis is no different when it comes to developing a plan to win. At most, doubles partners tell each other on the spot where they are hitting to, and I call this surface planning. Yes, there are plays to run, command poaches and serves to the weaker sides that are part of the basics of smart surface planning. What I recommend for players/partners to do is to challenge themselves to come up with a more thought-provoking tennis system, one that will be active throughout an entire match, tournament and career. There are reasons why doubles teams stay in the top, and it is not because of luck or physical skill, but mostly because of mental planning with strategic systems that keep them in check on the court.

Controlling doubles play: Doubles play needs to be looked at as a "Mental Giant." The doubles players have to move smartly and move with a higher degree of anticipation than the other opponents. Knowing opponents and how they move will help generate great anticipation as players begin to know where and when their opponents like to hit their shots. But before a pair of doubles partners can enter that realm, they must establish a system based on knowing where their opponents are going to hit the ball. I call my system, the "Triangle System."

What is the "Triangle System?" The triangle system is based upon offense, defensive and neutral plays at which a ball is set at a particular location and hit to another location based on the degree of change. What is the triangle offense? If a player (player 1) playing directly ahead is deep at the baseline, the player at the net (player 2) will be moving towards the net. However, more importantly, player 2 hit the best shot to set up player 1. If the offense (player 2) just hit the ball back crosscourt and nothing changed, then they are not playing doubles. The player that is on the baseline needs to always be setting up the player at the net which their shot selection. This is how this system generates offensive plays on the court. A regular poaching system also consists of movements such as partner lobs over the person ahead of them from the baseline. The player at the net automatically should switch as well as their opponents, as they are going to retrieve the lob. This puts team A and team B in the reset position, which is great for both sides as a defensive lob was hit by team A to reset the point.

"The Set Up"

There are times that players are going to play doubles with a partner that does not move, and that is okay. It is okay because they know where their partner is going to be, so they can control the point to where their partner is at the net. A player will need to get his or her double a volley at the net for a put away. Of course, the player has to avoid the obvious, which is the opponent at the net on the other side. Like volleyball, players get to rally before they can get a set shot. Players can tell their partners to not move and to stay up at the net and wait for the put away. I like to call this the "waiting game." The balls may move too fast, so a player cannot always move from side to side to cover the middle and the line when he or she is the middle man. It is up to the person on the baseline to rally to dictate the point and prevent the opposing side of getting a chance to set before that team does. However, the player at the net should sense a similar ball flight pattern coming from the opponent on the baseline. When able, the net player should always go before the opposing net player does. Always stay on the offense by setting up the net shot first. The team that goes for the offense the most will be the team that wins more doubles matches. It is very important to stay away from the drop shot and short angles in doubles. Yes, you can win a point here and there, but too often players play the low percentage shots, and the drop shot being one of those shots hinders a chance at winning. It is important to maintain consistent depth, if applicable. If a player does not have any other choice to hit, then a drop shot (before the service line) is okay to hit, because he or she is stuck without options. Always remember, doubles is about driving through your opponent, not acute angles and shot making abilities. With that being said, the lob will always be a player's friend.

Chapter 29 The Reset Button

When to reset. Resetting a point is the most crucial play in tennis. Without resetting the point, an opponent can run away with a match just as easily as saying, "I am done." Since tennis matches are like fighting matches, it is about strategically outlasting the opponent, and not just "I think I can hit a winner from this angle." Having the right mind set especially at both recreational and professional levels is crucial to one's mental toughness. The more robotic and natural tennis shots become, the less unforced errors and mistakes will be made. Errors generate a lot because players are not always sure where to hit or how to hit a shot they are trying for. If players are unsure, "Reset!" Making up the mind well in advance like clockwork is the first component to becoming an improved mental tennis player, instead of just trying to get the ball back into the court without reason. Even at the lowest level, where players are just trying to get it in, they will take longer to develop. Players should not fight against themselves in deciding what shots to hit or how they are supposed to win. If players are finding shot selection difficult, hit a ball that is deep and slow by the baseline to reset the point. Another way to reset is a slow angled ball to a side or corner. Remember what I said earlier about "time." The reset button is going to be the players' best shot to give them time to get back into the court/point. Recovering into the court with purpose and knowing what their reset button is will give them a chance to win points that they never thought they could win. Some good examples of reset shots are topspin or underspin lob, slice, drop shot and short angles. When players are able to reset, they will find themselves getting one more ball back, which is what it takes to win some matches and points.

Chapter 30 Understanding the Triangle System

There is only one reason for the triangle system and that is playing high percentage tennis. With the system comes the lowest part of the net to the deepest parts of the court with players' offensive, defensive and neutral plays. With this system, like poker, players are most likely to improve their winning percentage by playing those odds. By playing the system correctly, a player's game will improve tremendously.

The Golden Rule: There is only one exception to breaking the system, and that is the winner. If indeed a court opens up and there is a high percentage to end the point with a high percentage shot, players may take that chance and break the system for the winning shot. What happens if they get it or they miss? A player should not be going for the "winner" all the time, but he or she is allowed logical reasoning to go for a winner when the opportunity is greater than the systems percentage of gaining the point. The system is there to provide an opportunity to hit a winner or let the opponents create the error. Once a winning shot has already presented itself, a player is then allowed to go for the shot, "Golden Rule." Keep in mind players need to be able to take a change of direction when planning their "Golden Shot."

Fast play: Does this system really work in fast play or professional tennis? Absolutely, balls flying at one hundred miles per hour will change strategy, like a team playing double back or teams always poaching at the net. Keep in mind, there are going to be times such as when an opponent's serve is too good for the day or opponents are beating the other team even though that team is covering the higher percentage of the court all day long. A player should always play smart tennis, and what I mean by that is to figure out the opponent. It is very rare to find players who do not change tactics during a match. Keeping focused and driven on how to win until the match is over is crucial. From the opponents' footwork to the opponents' strengths and weaknesses "always think!" If an opponent is passing an opposing player after a number of tries in the same area, adjust! Again, keep in mind to always try to go back to the original game plan.

How to make sense of the system? Tennis works in two ways, players are playing towards their games, or they are playing into the hands of their opponents. It may not seem like it at the time, but spectators during a match can tell who is winning a match and who is controlling the points. The team who controls the points controls the outcome of the match. Yes, sometimes they will lose because of choices, pressure or fatigue, and then the controller becomes the controlled. In this system players are trying to get their opponents to play into their system of tennis to win free points.

How do I get free points from the system? The system has many aspects and one is the muscle memory of where to be at all the right times. Take pro basketball for example, they will get as many open shots off as they can, and the team that has the easiest time doing so, wins more outcomes. Granted there are times when players will have an off day or a team under-performs, but that is what we call sports. Sticking to the system, playing and improving the mental aspect of court positioning will increase players games bar none.

Chapter 31 Q & A

Q: Why would your system of teaching be good for me?

Brian: Great question, I designed my plays based on both logical and practical shots. If you take a close look, the shots that I choose for you to hit are all the ones that are deep with no short balls. The lines you hit are crosscourt and not down the line unless you have the court position to move forward to do so. This system is designed to be practical, and for you to practice intelligent tennis and not worry about unforced error and complex shots. Sticking with the system will improve your game dramatically both mentally and technically. Therefore, staying away from short balls gives you less scenarios of having aggressive shots hit by your opponent.

Q: How can I play good tennis when I am behind in a match?

Brian: "Comeback tennis" is one of the greatest times on the court. If you are a player that wants to win every point, then you will be wanting to understand "comeback tennis," because you are probably in this situation too often. I'll give you a comeback example to look for: "Reading the scores and playing it right." If you are down 2-3 or 3-4 or 4-5 with your opponent serving, you are in luck of getting a break back and win the set. If the opponent gets tight or changes his or her mental state, you will not only win the game but potentially the match, because your opponent knows that he or she let the opportunity slip away. It happens often that opponents domineer and mental states will change, and then players will start playing it safe, as they do not want to make errors. It is up to you to exploit those flaws and take over the match. You will notice your confidence and stroke production start to favor your game style. You then can run away with the match all because of that one game you broke back. It is crucial to remember that the match is never over until the last point is finished.

Q: Why are sequences better than my instincts?

Brian: I have heard that trusting your instincts is a good thing; it is possible that your instincts are correct most of the time, right? Tennis shots should never be hit at random based on what feels right at the particular time unless you have had the proper training. Perhaps you will notice a similar situation on court when you have hit the ball with a different solution than the time before. These are the instincts I would be most concerned about. There is always the best option to hit from your position and where the ball should go. Learn to know what shot to hit to reduce errors, then commit yourself with confidence. For instance, it is better to go into a tennis match with a game plan than to go into a match and try to wing it. It is no different when you break down shots and the decision-making process on court. If you trust your instincts too often, it will lead you down a harder path than one of physics and logical shot making. I will never tell you that you should never mix up your plans or use your variety. However, always play the smart move, whether it is the right time to use those other ideas, and understand the why factor to use them in those moments.

Q: I understand the system and it is not working.

Brian: Let us look at a few possibilities already before asking me to come watch you play. Reasons 1: I am playing it right, and it is not working. This is a famous case of when players think they are playing into the system, but are not. I watched a doubles match recently, I saw numerous times that the person (player1) at the net hit a volley to the diagonal player (player 2), who was sitting waiting to volley. This allowed player 2 to control the point and hit the ball up the middle for a winner.

I ask him (player 1), "Why are you hitting it to him?" He responded, "Because I'm trying to hit it at him and end the point". I see these issues all the time where the logic of a winning shot overrides the logical outcome of the point. It is important to remember that you should never trade your offense play for another teams' offensive play (net vs. net). For instance, when you play a game of chess, you never want to drag your queen down to the other side of the board and say check just because you think you have your opponent on the run. Chess players like tennis players need to think long-term, which means both the point I am playing, and the outcome of the match. By giving the other opponent the ball at net is almost like saying, "I am aggressive; let us see if you are aggressive." If it were myself playing, why would I give a shark a chance to bite back, when a fish is dangling on the baseline? Hitting the ball through the middle or back deep gives you at the net the most aggressive tactic on the court. Remember what I said earlier about the golden rule. Since hitting the opponent at net is not producing winners, it is not allowed to be hit there.

Q: Once I learn the system and others know the system, does my opponent figure me out, so I will not get the highest percentage to win a match now since my opponent and I are even?

Brian: Absolutely not, though there is truth in the sense that players and teams are always trying to work out their own strategy and learn their opponents' as well as they can to get an edge. However, playing the highest percentage tennis will make them adapt, and once they do, you actually have more control than before. Take doubles for example, it is a higher percentage to go cross-court, but opponents will poach, and when they do, down the line is open. "Remember golden rule!" If the court is open going diagonally and the opponent is blocking the down the line shot, you have the highest percentage to stay in the point, and there is great opportunity to set up your partner.

Two other quick notes here: 1) Your partner should always switch when you hit down the line, and your partner will be in an offensive position. 2) If a switch did not happen, and it comes back to you on the baseline, then a deep topspin lob crosscourt is still a great reset option to keep your partner in position. This will maximize your opportunity within the offensive triangle system.

Chapter 32 Tennis Sequences

Whether you have read and understood the meaning of the system, here is a visual of how tennis can be played with the right shot selections. Here I have tennis sequences that you should memorize when you go on court to play singles or doubles. Look for yourself, and say, "Am I playing into the sequence or am I missing my opportunities?" It is important to realize that each sequence is designed that you as "number one" should know your options when the ball is returned into the court. The sequence is designed to play structured points and to teach players to know what to expect and when to expect it.

"First Sequence"

The numbers represent where the player contacts the ball on the court. The arrows
represent the ball traveling from one location to the other. For instance, a player hits a ball at player two. As player two was unable to return the ball

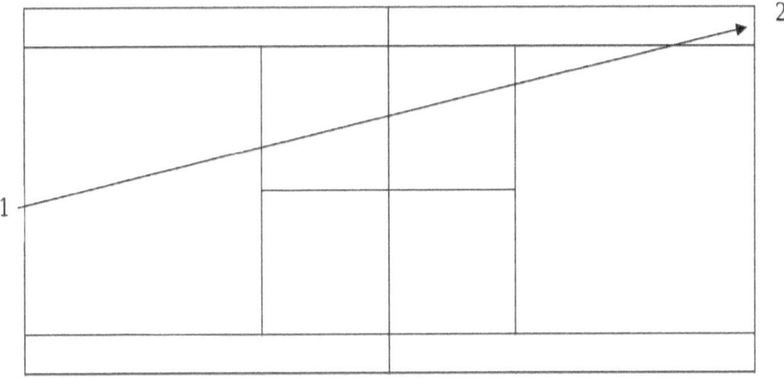

back, there is no return arrow.

Three Ball Strike # 1 Cross Court Finish: The design shows when ball is returned and player hits a winner into open court based on court positioning. **The sequence below shows a cross court winner from the baseline hit after serving. 1) Serving cross court 2) Return down the line 3) Hitting cross court to open court.**

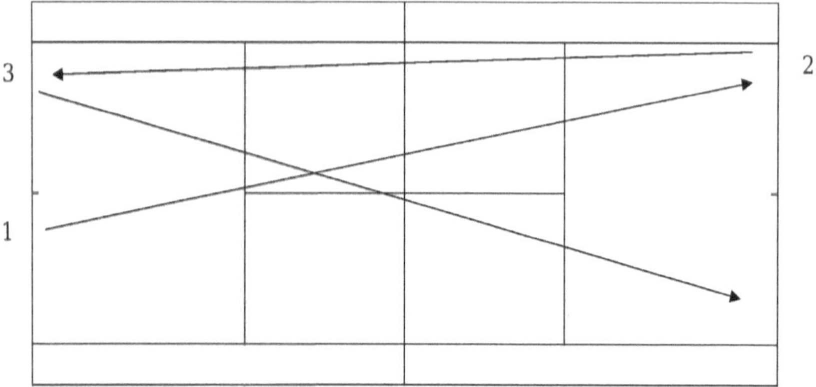

Three Ball Strike #2 Cross Court Finish: Getting set up for a high bounce or even a ball in the strike zone can result in a winner or an unforced error from your opponent on your second hit to the open court. This is a basic one- two combo that allows you to hit into the open court for a winner or gets your opponent on the run for a future opportunity. **The sequence below shows a cross court hit into the open court after receiving a short ball from the opponent. 1) Serving diagonal 2) Returning up the middle 3) Hitting to the open court.**

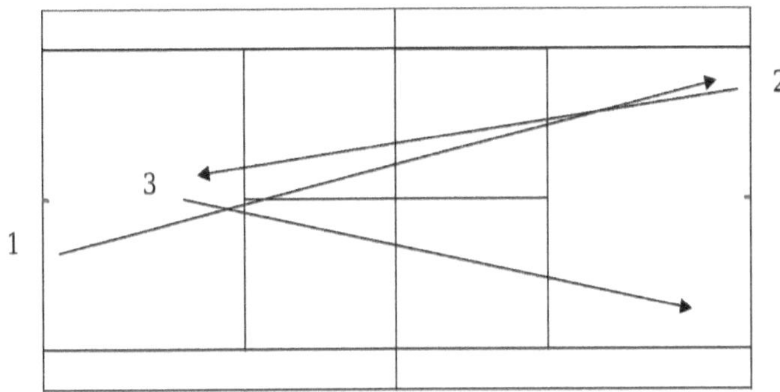

Three Ball Strike # 3 Cross Court Finish: Hitting a volley into the open court can lead to an easy winner or force an error from your opponent. **The sequence below shows a volley being hit cross court after a serve. 1) Serving cross court 2) Return down the line 3) Volley cross court.**

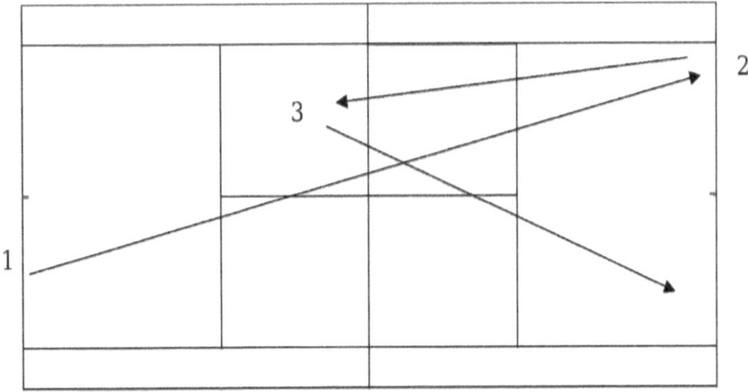

Three Ball Cross Court: Look to hit cross-court to force an unforced error. If you can pull your opponent off the court with your forehand, you can possibly land a future winner. Use this shot not only for winners but too create opportunities from your opponent. **The sequence below shows a continuation of multiple hits cross-court at an approximate zero degree change of angle. 1) Serving cross court   2) Returning cross court 3) Hitting cross court.**

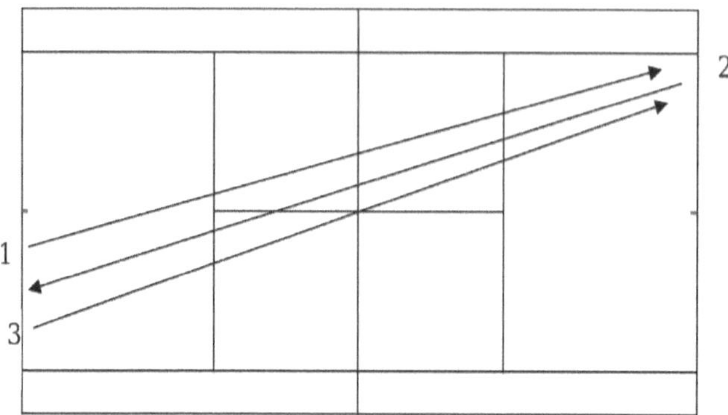

Three Ball Volley Reset: Unlike the Striking Volley. A player can use the court position to force an error. You can also give yourself a second volley. Sometimes, a player does not want to hit the first volley cross-court and will play the first ball back to the opponent for later shot (Reset). **The sequence below shows a player hitting the ball back to the returner to either create an error or earn a second opportunity to hit an open winner crosscourt volley. 1) Serving cross court 2) Return down the line   3) Volley down the line.**

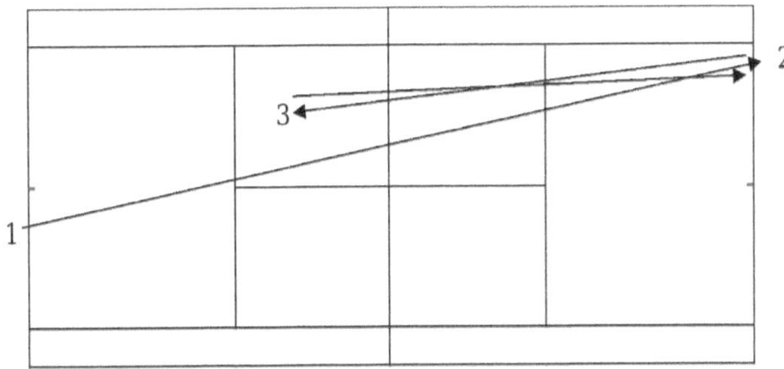

Five Ball V Cross Strike: If for any reason that your crosscourt winner on 3 ball striking did not produce a winner, you must quickly recover to the other side of the court to number 5 for the next volley. Sometimes your volley at 3 will produce a defensive hit from your opponent, which will result in a short ball. You will still finish at hit number 5, which finishes the point. . **The sequence below shows 1) Serving cross court 2) Return down the line 3) Volley cross court into open court 4) Hit down the line 5) Volley cross court into open court.**

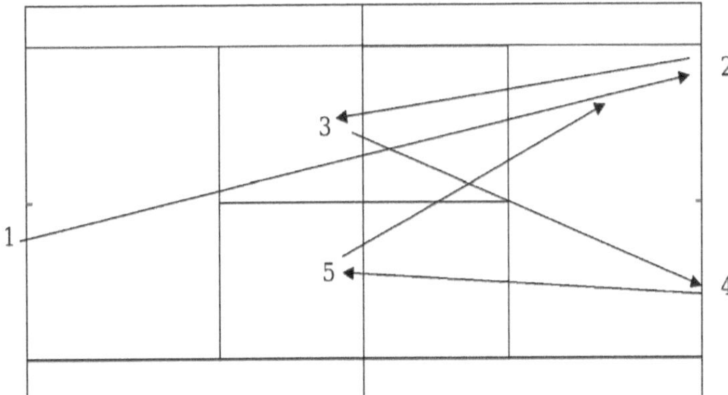

Five Ball Strike with Volley Reset 1: There will be times that a player must set up their position before using a finishing shot. Utilizing court position and time, this play design helps see the point through. **The sequence below shows 1) Serving cross court 2) Return down the line 3) Volley down the line 4) Hit down the line 5) Volley cross-court into open court.**

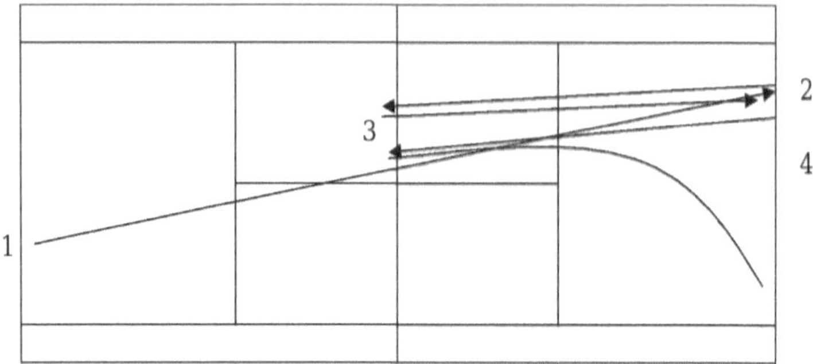

Five Ball Reset Design 2: This design also shows that even when your opponent is at the net, the tactics stay the same in order to achieve resetting the point. Since the opponent came up to the net, we can reset on the 5th Ball. **The sequence shows 1) Serving cross court 2) Returning cross court 3) Hitting cross court 4) Volleying down the line 5) Lobbing cross court.**

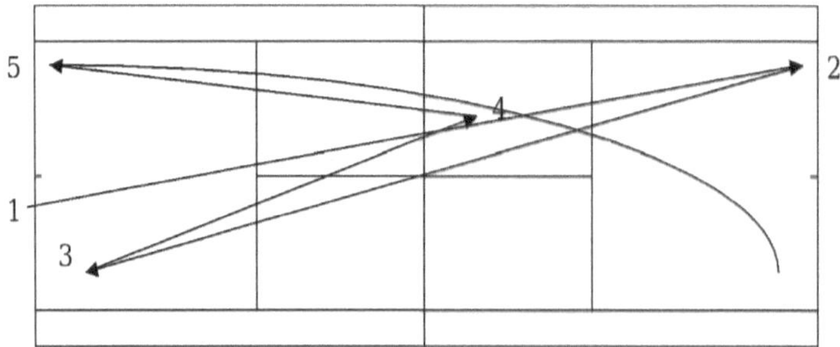

Five Ball with Volley Reset 2: There will be times that a player must set up their position before using a finishing shot. Utilizing court position and time, this design below shows the point with proper court position. **The sequence below shows 1) Serving cross court 2) Return cross court 3) Volley down the line 4) Hit to the middle 5) Volley cross court to open court.**

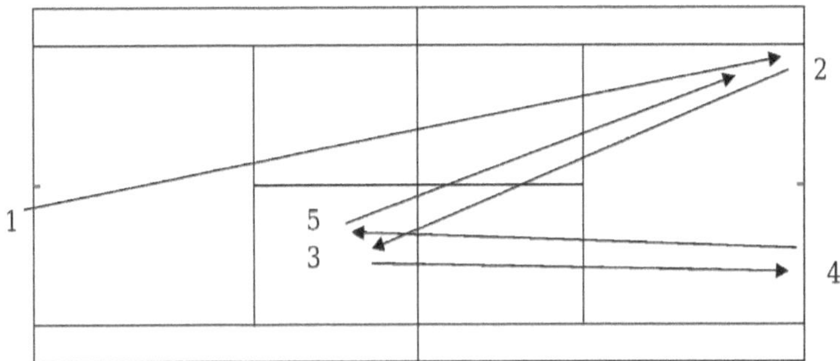

Five Ball Reset: If there were any point where your offensive play must turn into defensive play, a wide forehand that you cannot get much power on would be one of those shots. A player must be able to give himself or herself time to recover back into the court with a high topspin lob to generate time to recover back into the court. **The sequence below shows 1) Serving cross court 2) Return cross court   3) Hit cross court 4) Hit cross court 5) Lob cross court.**

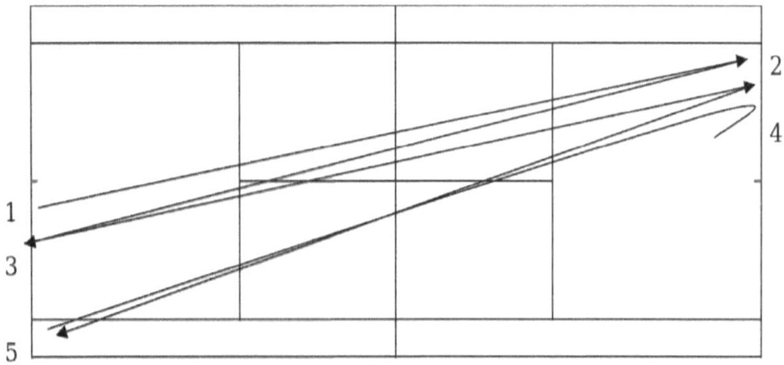

Fifth Ball Reset # 2: If a player hits a powerful stroke up the line and you have a hard time running it down, utilize the defensive topspin lob to get you back into proper court positioning. If you have limited time to only slice it without a lob, your opponent will probably have an approach or an easy volley. Lobbing the ball gets you in resetting position to start the point back over again in neutral position. **The sequence below shows 1) Serving cross court 2) Return cross court 3) Hit cross court 4) Hit down the line 5) Lob cross court.**

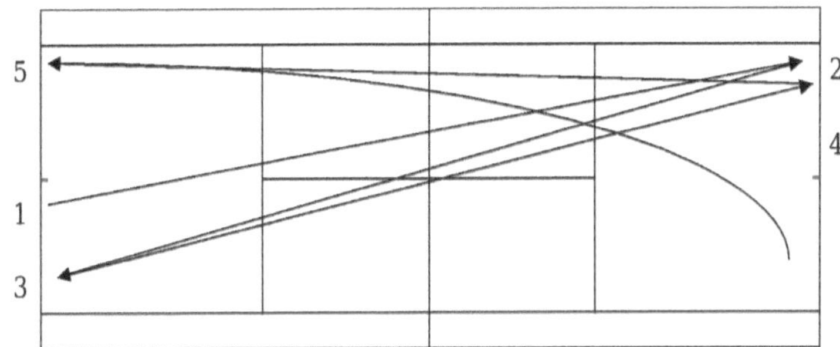

Seven Ball Strike with one Volley Reset: This may look like many volleys, but the first volley is designed for court positioning. Given the player has a weaker backhand; you can volleys back to the opponent on the second volley #5 if hit number 3 was unsuccessful for a winner. You do not always have to go crosscourt on number 5 on the first try if you feel that the ball that was hit in your comfort zone for an easy volley. **The sequence below shows 1) Serving cross court 2) Return cross court 3) Volley down the line 4) Hit down the line 5) Volley down the line 6) Hit down the line 7) Volley cross court into open court.**

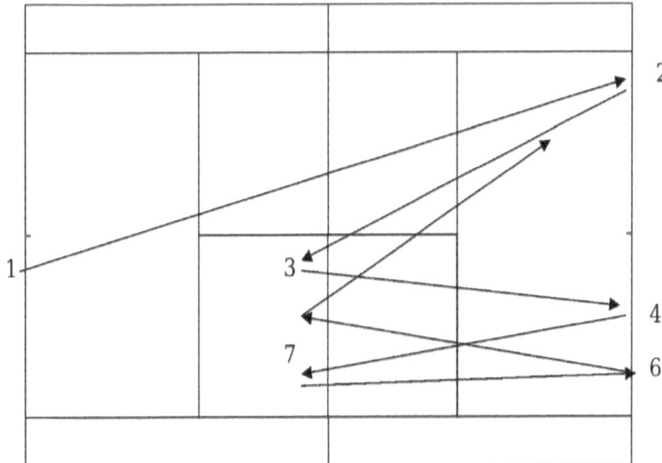

Seven Ball Volley/Net Pressure Option: Taking into account that your opponent has a weak backhand, you can allow yourself the ability to force an error. Three shots are the max that you want to give your opponent for their weakness. This can also be labeled as "resetting" since you are resetting your opponent on a consistent basis and have advantage with court position. The benefit is that you are volleying the ball close to the 0 degree. Nevertheless, make no mistake, if you have an easy put away volley, you most certainly can finish out the point cross-court towards number 2. **The sequence below shows 1) Serving cross court 2) Return cross court 3) Volley down the line 4) Hit down the line 5)Volley down the line 6) Hit down the line 7) Volley down the line 8) Unforced error by opponent.**

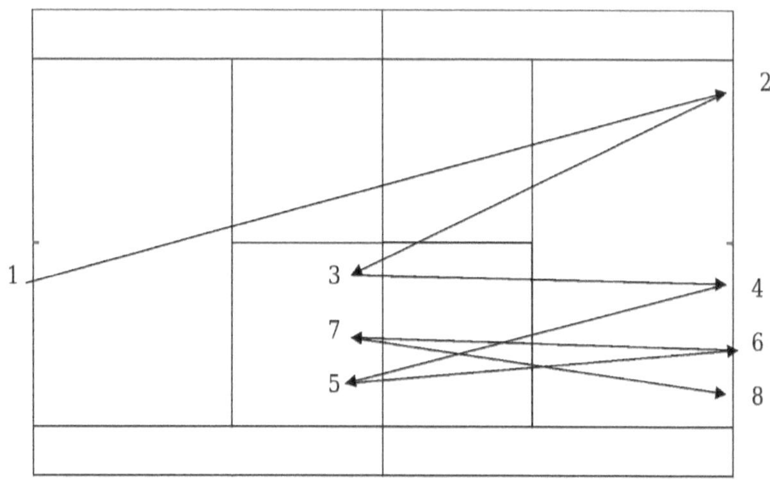

Multiple Resets: It is not too often that long points go on enough to where you will need to reset. However, there are matches where power is a rarity and points will go on with limited errors or winners because of the lack of pace on the ball. When this is the case, we will see multiple resets within a point. Even when a person hits a lob, the hit that will be returned back will be another topspin lob. **The sequence below shows 1) Serving cross court 2) Lob/ reset return cross court 3) Lob/reset hit cross court 4) Hit down the middle 5) Volley cross court to open court 6) Hit down the line 7) Volley down the line 8) Lob/reset cross court 9) Lob.**

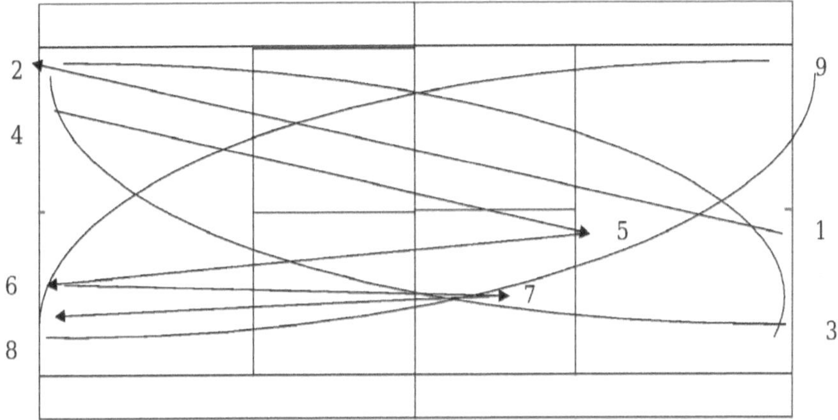

Doubles Ball Strike 1: A very simple doubles strategy that implies setting up your partner for a winner or forcing an error from your opponent. The opposing doubles partner is at the next on the service line (x). It is necessary to go towards the middle to spread the court and hit with the greatest margin of error. **The sequence below shows 1) Serving cross court 2) Return down the line 3) Volley in the middle between the opposing players.**

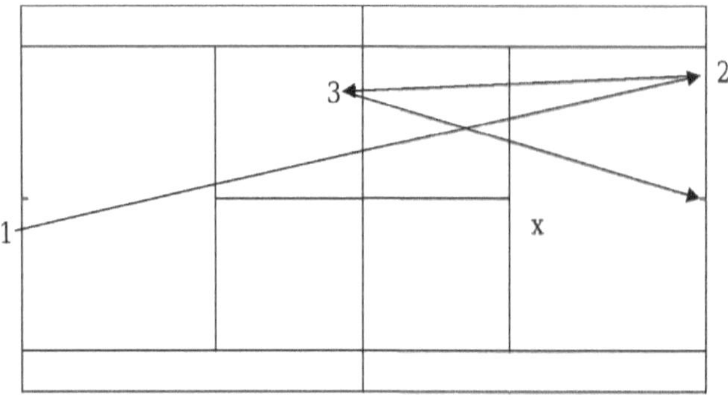

Doubles Ball strike with 1 Reset: There will be times when hitting the ball back to the baseline player is significant for timing and playability. There is no strategically wise fault to not be ready in the same position for a second chance to go up the middle. Some returners can return a serve very well, and it is up to the net player to react very quickly and be ready to execute on the next ball up the middle. **The sequence below shows 1) Serving cross court 2) Return down the line 3) Volley down the line 4) Hit down the line 5) Volley in the middle.**

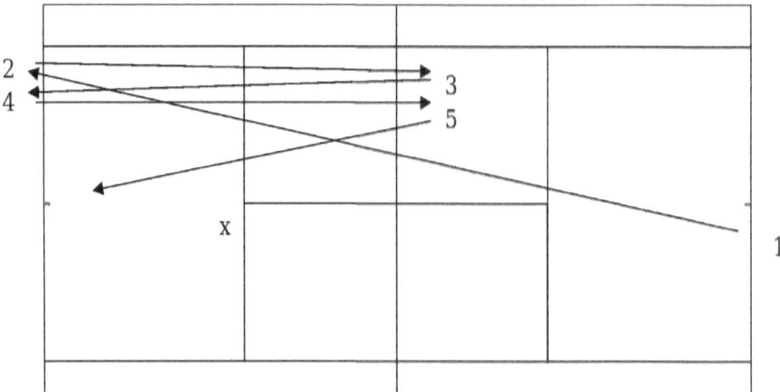

Doubles 5 Ball Strike Setup: Setting up your partner to win the point is the best thing you can do besides forcing an unforced error from your opponent. Do not let your partner approach at random. If the ball is out of the net persons control to win the point, you do not know the angle of the next ball unless it is coming really soft or slow. Your best bet is to wait for the opponent to hit late or hit a ball he cannot control well. Your partner will then hit into the open court to win the point. **The sequence below shows 1) Serving cross court 2) Return cross court 3) Hit cross court 4) Soft/late hit down the line   5) Volley in the middle between the opposing players.**

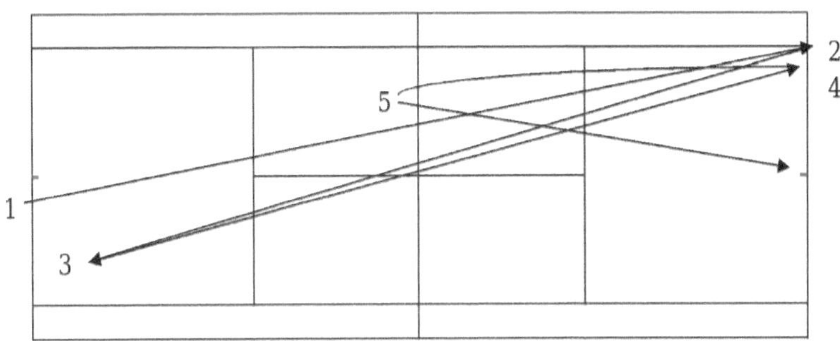

Doubles Five Ball Strike: Like the 3 ball strike, the 5 ball is the one that will take an extra hit to finish the point. It is important in doubles to not engage the other net person as that person is a distraction to yourself. The court position of the ball is best played into the hands of the opposing baseline player. If the ball was hit to the x. The x player would go up the middle between hits 1 and 5 to win the point. It is important for the net player to read the court and finish the job by rallying out the baseline hitter with their volleys. **The sequence below shows 1) Serving cross court 2) Return down the line 3) Volley in the middle between opposing players 4) Hit down the middle 5) Volley cross court to open court away from opponents.**

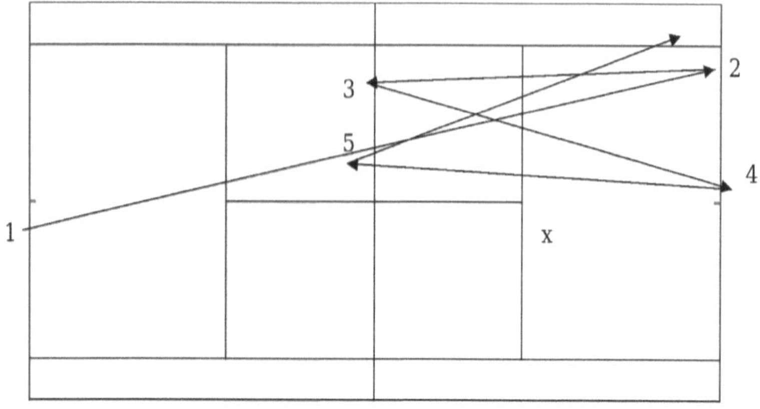

Doubles Eight Ball Reset: This 8-ball reset is when the opposing team is putting pressure you. A reset lob is significant to get from defensive to offensive, and the lob is a clear option to reset since both opposing players are at the net. The baseline returner has the most court to work with, and this is one of those moments you can use the lob to reset. **The sequence below shows 1) Serving cross court   2) Return cross court 3) Hit crosscourt 4) Hit down the line 5) Volley in the middle 6) Hit cross court   7) Volley cross court 8) Lob cross court.**

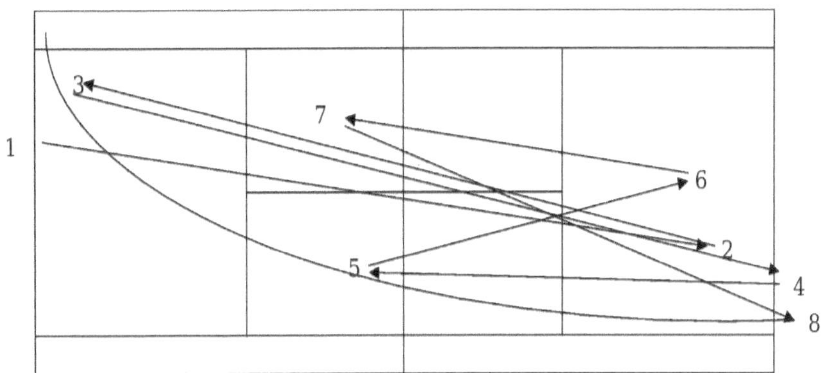

Double Back/ Infinity Reset: Playing double back in doubles, players have to prepare for balls that reset multiple times during a point. It is important to always try to set up your partner in doubles. If you are getting beat by the opposing teams net player, utilize the lob to reset the points. There is also no harm in lobbing deep (past the service line) cross court. Remember, changing the angle during a point can lead to possible errors and the opponent's ability to hit into the open court. If the player hits down the line to X, X can lob over your partner's head at the net or hit through the middle, which would make us fall out of position. Therefore, keep hitting cross court until you set your partner up and reset the point with a lob when you have to. **The sequence below shows 1) Serving cross court 2) Return cross court 3) Hit cross court + Infinity 4) Hit cross court + Infinity.**

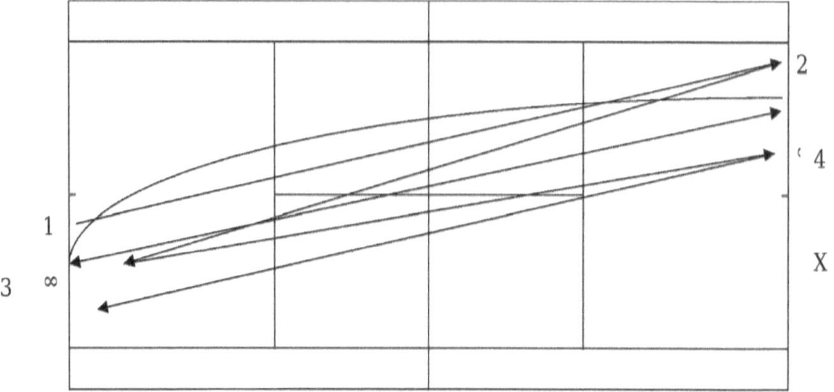

Doubles Returning to Reset: In doubles, there will be times where you are counter punching or playing the defensive stance to get into a point. It is here when resetting the point back to the start is ok. The defensive options are going middle or lobbing which are options 2 and option 3 since we are getting a quick volley from hit #3. Drop shots are extremely rare in this circumstance. It is best to reset and get back into the point by involving the opposing baseline player. The reason we are going back to the start with option 1 is because the middle would be covered by opposing player that hit # 3 hence, he or she would have moved closer to the net and is now covering the middle ball. **The sequence below shows 1) Serving cross court 2) Return down the line 3) Volley cross court 4) Option 1 Volley down the line, Option 2 Volley middle, Option 3 Lob volley cross court.**

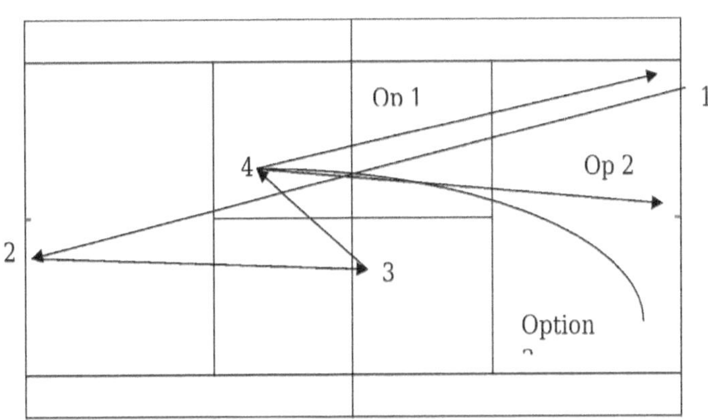

Op 1
Op 2
Option
1
2
3
4

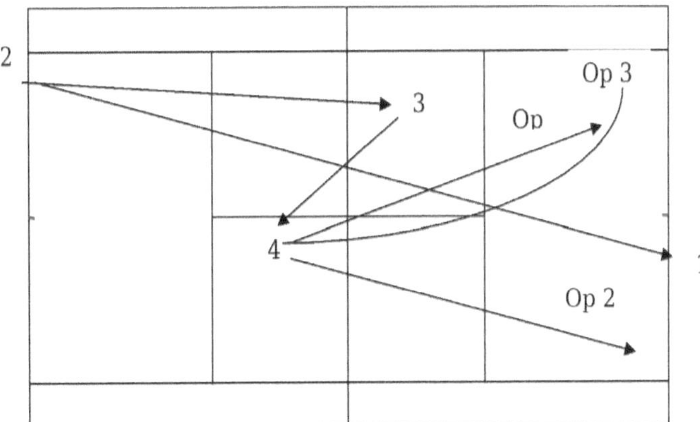

2
Op 3
Op
3
Op 2
1
4

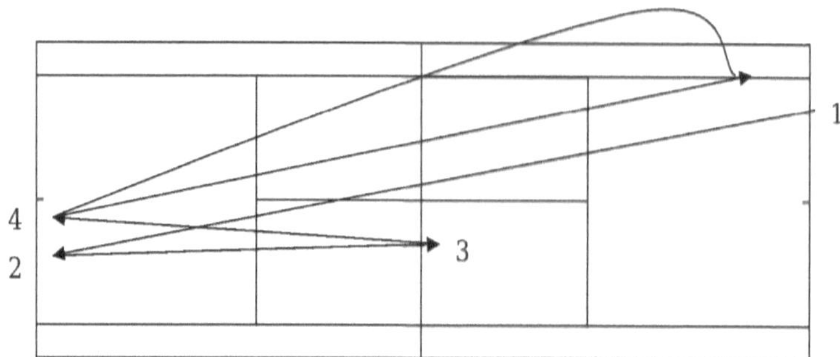

Doubles Baseline Returning & Resetting: Sometimes serves are hit so big, and you have to cover the middle because the ball is going to the opposing team net player. If this is the case, cover the middle shot and reset the ball back to the baseline player with a lob or a hit to give your team another chance to start the point over to get into an offensive position. **The sequence below shows 1) Serving cross court 2) Return down the line 3) Volley in the middle 4) Hit cross court or reset lob cross court.**

Doubles Returning 6 Ball Reset: This reset is a very important during a point that is getting defensive. This design shows all players on the court have to eventually move to stay in proper court positioning. The last reset will force the returning partner to move to cover the net. The serving team looking to end the point has to decide whether to switch after the returning team lobs ball #6. Ball #6 would be the baseliner's defensive lob after scrambling to reach the ball after hit #5 did not hit hard enough to secure the winning shot. **The sequence below shows 1) Serving cross court 2) Return cross court 3) Hit cross court 4) Hit down the line 5) Volley in the middle 6) Lob or reset cross court.**

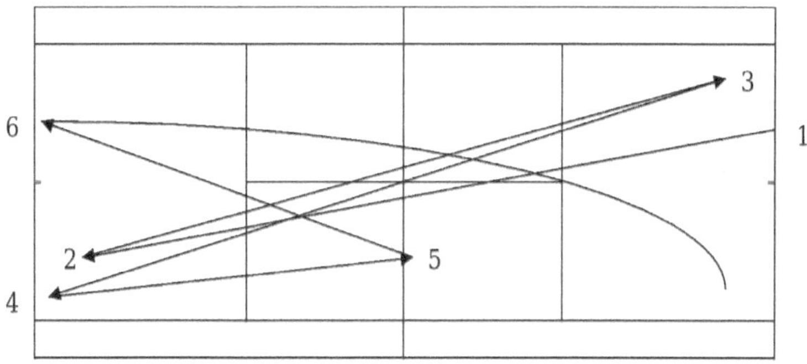

(Δ)Singles Play 1 Defense/P2 Neutral/P3 Offense: (Op: Opponent)

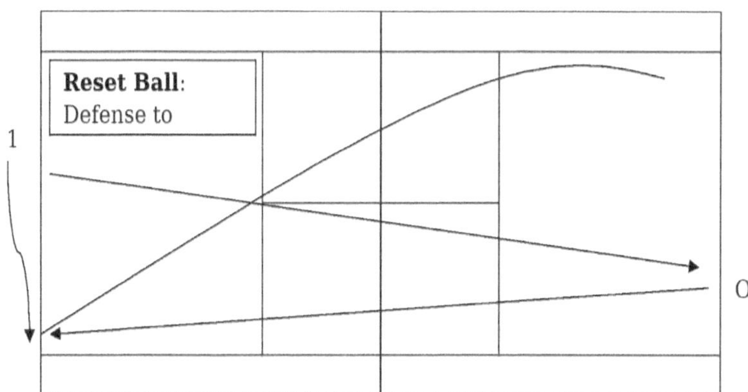

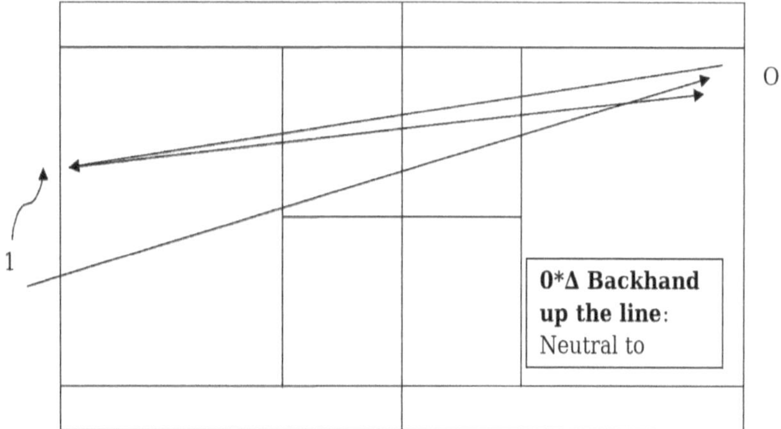

1
0
0*Δ Backhand up the line:
Neutral to

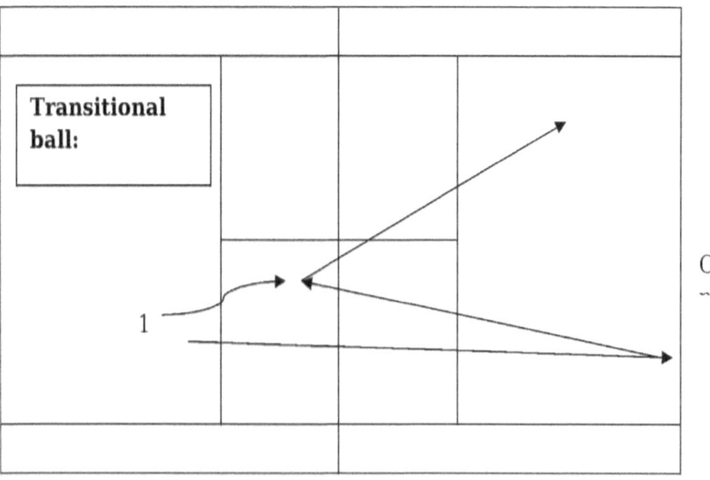

Transitional ball:
1
0

(Δ) Neutral/Offensive/Defensive (Op: Opponent)

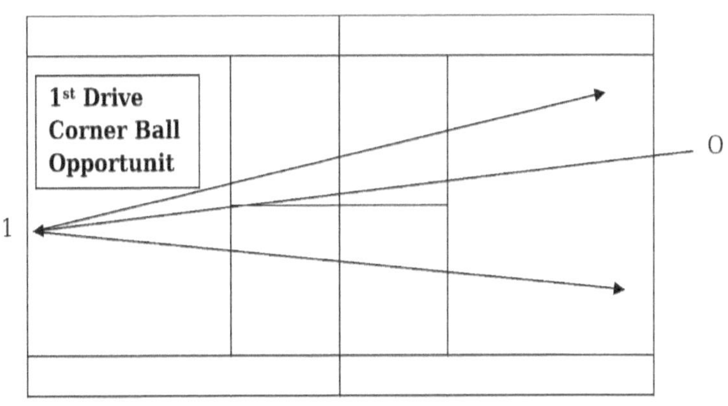

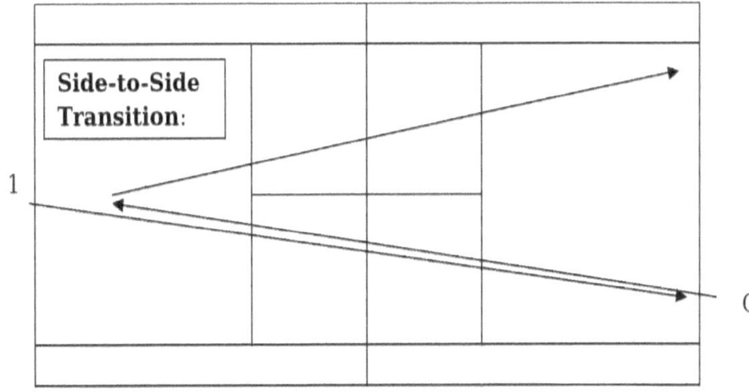

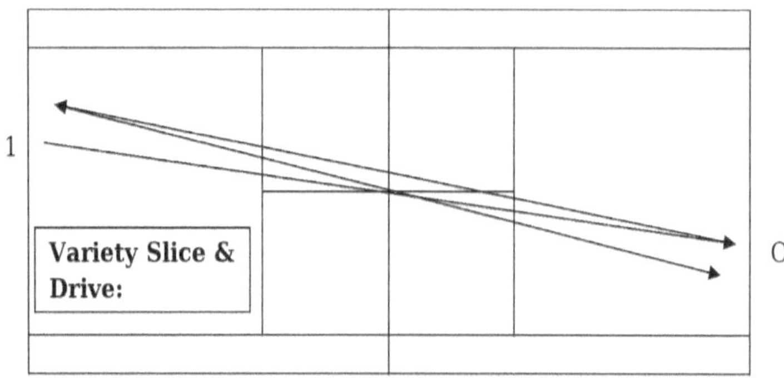

(Δ) Neutral/ Offensive/Defensive (Op: Opponent)

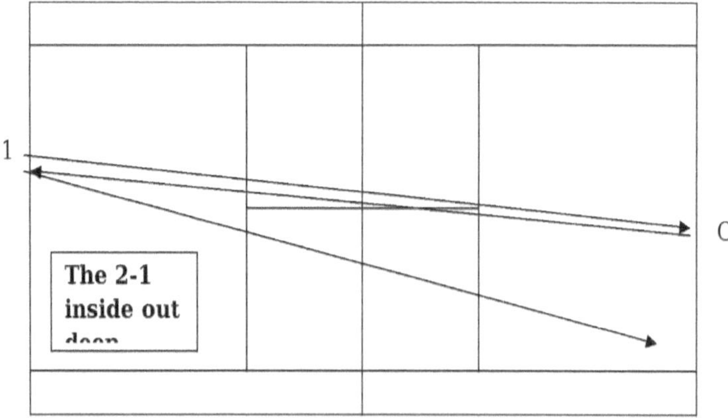

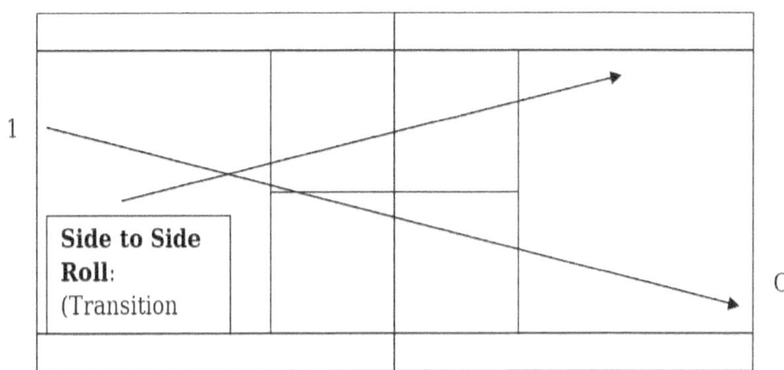

1
Side to Side Roll:
(Transition
0

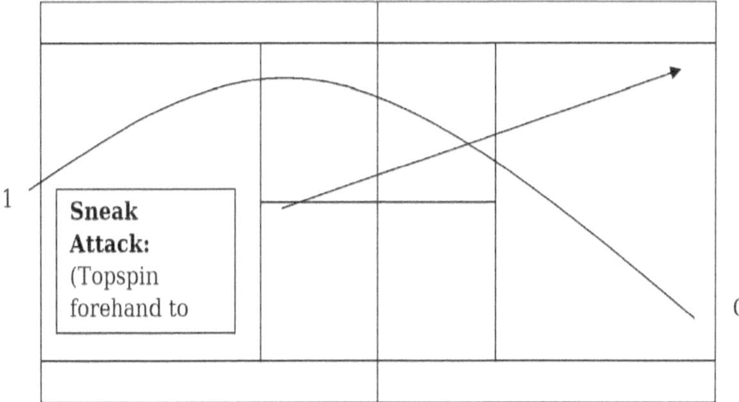

1
Sneak Attack:
(Topspin forehand to
0

(Δ) Triangle System:

Court Positioning by Quadrants & Middle Coverage

1) **Never Go Quad 4** unless overhead possibility.
2) **Quad 1 and 2** will keep you being an **obstacle** and get set up at net.
3) The **normal 45s** are from **quad 2 and 3** when your side has the ball and looking for defensive or neutral moves.
4) Be aggressive on serves **and start closer in quad 1** to force opponents to change directions, look to **move quad 1 to quad 1 often.**
   Ex: Serves to middle go quad 1. If wide serve on either side, quad 2.

4	2	
3	1	
3	1	
4	2	

(Δ) Middle Coverage (Continued)

1) Cover the middle as often as possible.
2) Higher percentage of play through the middle.
3) Play doubles as if you are playing singles with a partner.

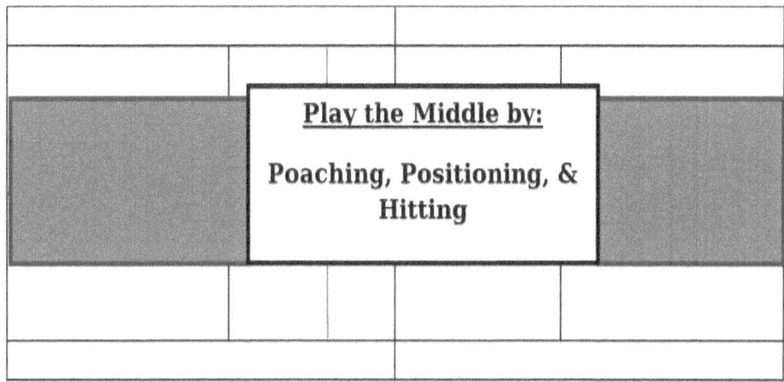

(Δ)Doubles Serve Play: Neutral Serve Plays (Wide, Middle, & T)

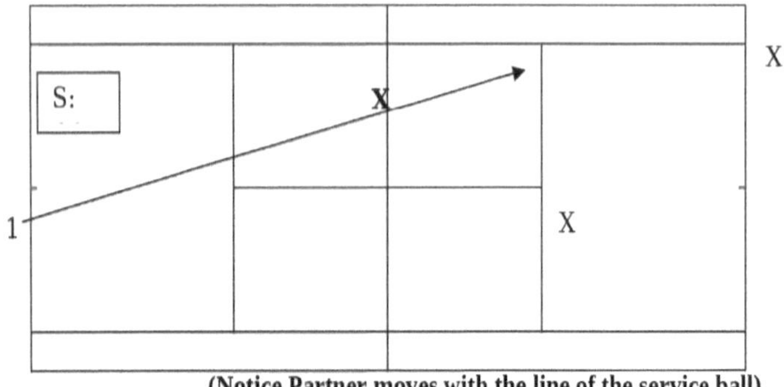

(Notice Partner moves with the line of the service ball)

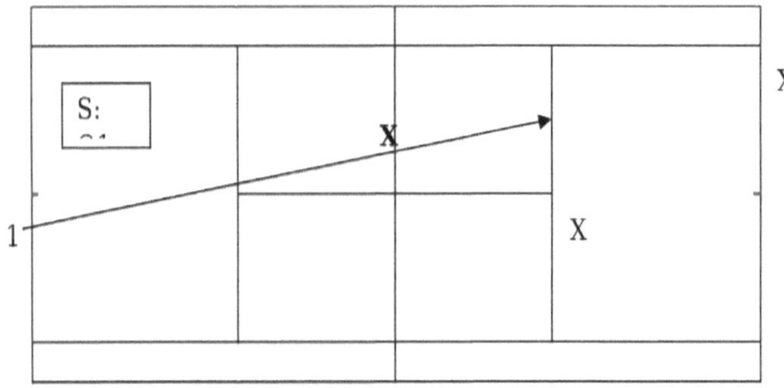

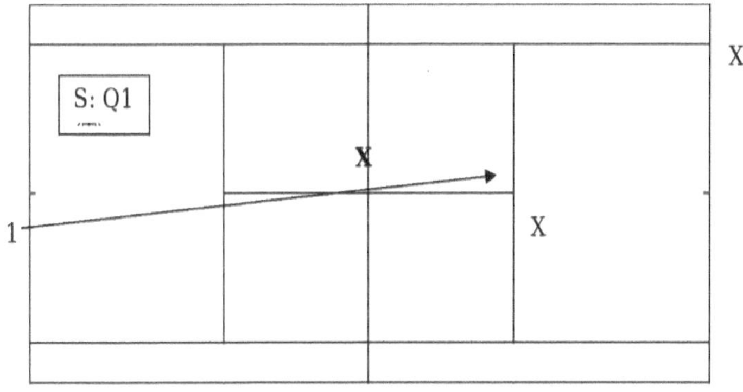

(Δ)Doubles Serve Play: Defensive Serve Plays (Wide, T, Middle)

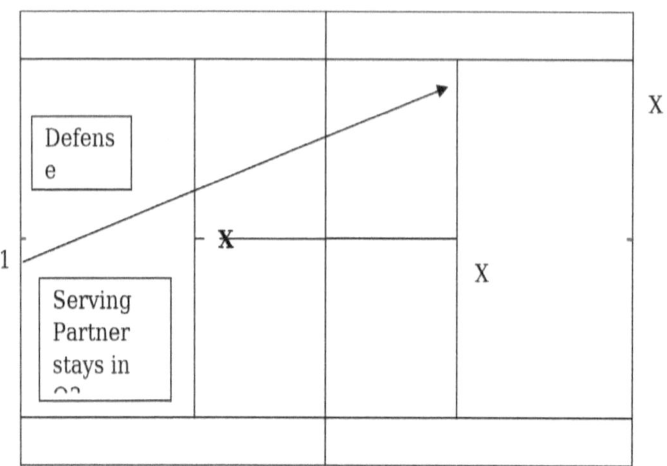
1
Defense
Serving Partner stays in Q3
X
X
X

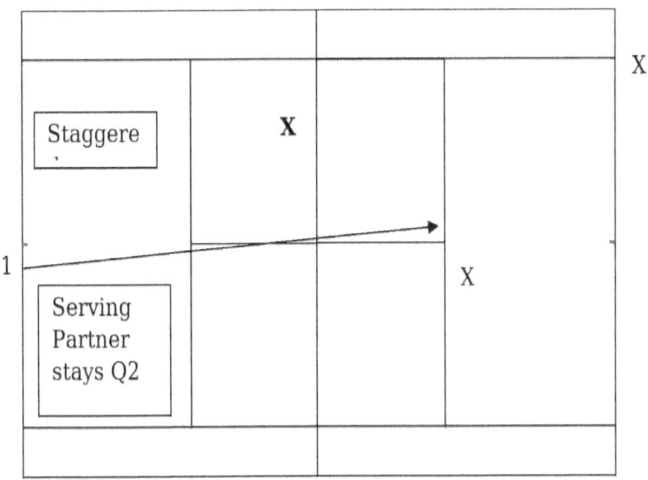
Staggere
Serving
Partner
stays Q2
X
X
X
1

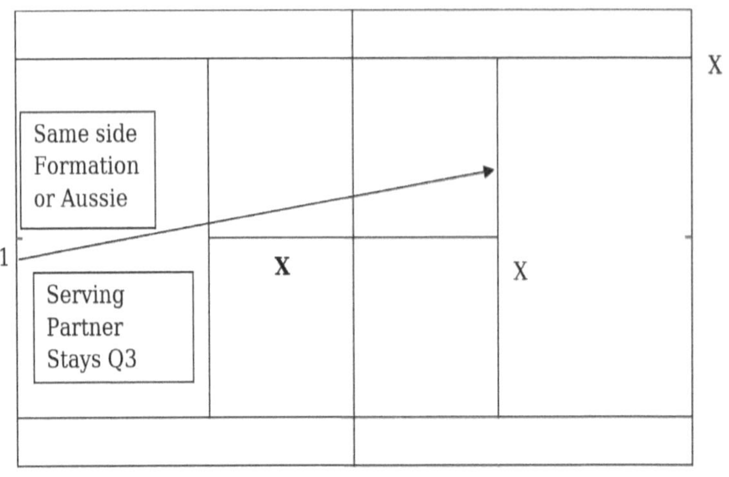

Doubles Serve Play: Offensive Serve Plays (Wide, T, T)

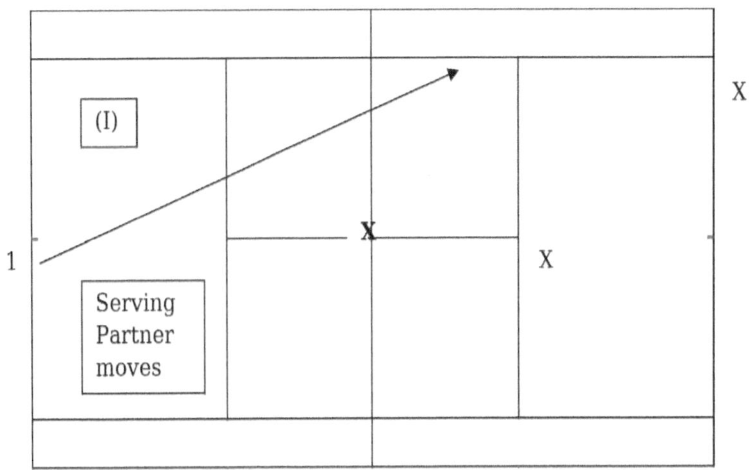
(I)
Serving
Partner
moves
1
X
X
X

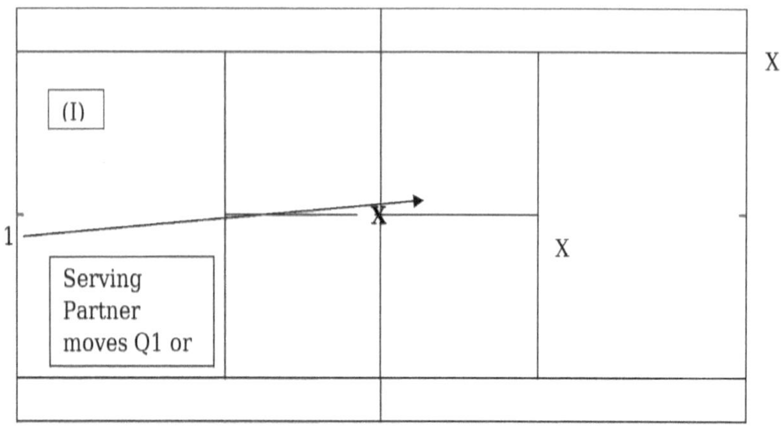
(I)
X
1
X
Serving
Partner
moves Q1 or
X

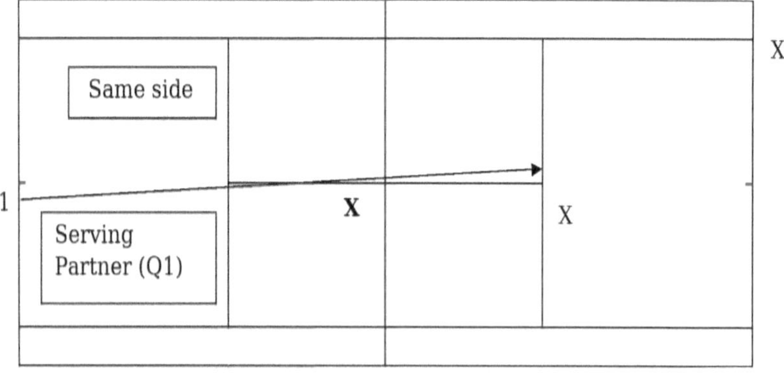
X
Same side
1
X
X
Serving
Partner (Q1)